THE ~VERY BEST OF MONTY PYTHON

methuen

THE VERY BEST OF MONTY PYTHON

SELECTED AND INTRODUCED BY
JOHN CLEESE, TERRY GILLIAM, ERIC IDLE,
TERRY JONES AND MICHAEL PALIN

WRITTEN AND CONCEIVED BY
GRAHAM CHAPMAN, JOHN CLEESE
TERRY GILLIAM, ERIC IDLE
TERRY JONES AND MICHAEL PALIN

Published by Methuen 2006
10 9 8 7 6 5 4 3 2 1

First published in Great Britain by
Methuen Publishing Ltd
11–12 Buckingham Gate
London SW1E 6LB
www.methuen.co.uk

Methuen Publishing Limited Reg. No. 3543167

ISBN 10: 0-413-77615-8
ISBN 13: 978-0-413-77615-0

A CIP catalogue record for this title is available from the British Library

Design by Katy Hepburn, Alun Evans and Crispin Rose-Innes

Printed and bound in Slovenia
Compass Press

CONTENTS

SELECTED
BY
TERRY
GILLIAM

WITH A PREFACE BY ERIC IDLE

INTRODUCTI^ON

Dear reader, or browser (if you happen to be one of those cheap bastards that hang about in bookstores fingering the goods, foxing the pages, scuffing the dust jackets with no intention of ever shelling out) here is your chance to take part in the greatest historical event of our age – SAVING THE COMEDY RAINFORESTS.

As you know, they are being RAVAGED at an ever increasing rate by GREEDY COMEDIANS who have no interest in the sustainable maintenance of these riches – interested only in the QUICK GAG, the SNAPPY ONE-LINER, the SMART-ARSE PUNCH LINE. Do they ever consider how long it takes for a good joke to mature? No! Their only concern is their own immediate gratification, satisfying the TV audience's insatiable demand for NEW LAUGHS!

Well, here is your chance to help.

All the material in this book is GUARANTEED TO BE OLD! RECYCLED! Old, recycled comic material from the legendary Monty Python team. NOTHING NEW! Not a single new joke or idea has been sacrificed for this tome.

By buying this book you are helping to preserve a FUNNY, LAUGH-FILLED FUTURE for your children – assuming they don't die when global warming melts the icecaps and causes the seas to rise and drown Norfolk and other low-lying areas of Britain including that bit of land where Sizewell B is located, causing unparalleled leakages of deadly radioactive material which will wipe out all the sea life around this island forever, or maybe, even, cause A NUCLEAR DISASTER THAT WILL MAKE CHERNOBYL LOOK LIKE A TEDDY BEAR'S PICNIC!!!!.

OK, buying this book is, in the long term, absolutely pointless. But, if you are one of those cheap bastards browsing your way through these pages, count yourself lucky – this hasn't cost you a penny.

If, however, you've already paid for the book, see page 59.

T.G. February 2000

JOIN THE **BBC** TODAY!

Deep down, let's face it, all of us hate
foreigners. It's quite natural when one lives
in such a beautiful and perfect country as
our own to hate and loathe those greasy-haired
snivelling toadies from Europe and beyond.
What worries me is that sometimes this hatred
is so deep down that many of us forget about
it, and instead of hitting Frenchmen and
letting Dagos' tyres down, we are buying
garlic-smelling French cars and eating filthy
chunks of Wop dough in stinking Pizza
parlours. Now I'm not saying that we should
go out and burn down the nearest Eye-tie,
Chink, Froggie or Pakki restaurant — I think
the army should be doing that — but if we are
going to keep this lovely country of ours
beautiful, clean and deeply religious, we must
remember that the Young Bigots Club is only a
phone call away. They will come round at a
moment's notice and tread on packets of
Gauloises and throw Grundig equipment down the
lavatory. Remember, tolerance is a great
British virtue — let's not waste it on Yids,
Polacks, Wops, Krauts and Arabs.

Col. Sir Harry McWhirter M.C.C.,
Chairman The Bloody Bigots Club

THE MEANING OF LIFE

Why are we here, what is life all about?
Is God really real, or is there some doubt?
Well tonight we're going to sort it all out,
For tonight it's the Meaning of Life.

What's the point of all these hoax?
Is it the chicken and egg time, are we just yolks?
Or perhaps we're just one of God's little jokes,
Well *ça c'est* the Meaning of Life.

Is life just a game where we make up the rules
While we're searching for something to say
Or are we just simply spiralling coils
Of self-replicating DNA?

What is life? What is our fate?
Is there Heaven and Hell? Do we reincarnate?
Is mankind evolving or is it too late?
Well tonight here's the Meaning of Life.

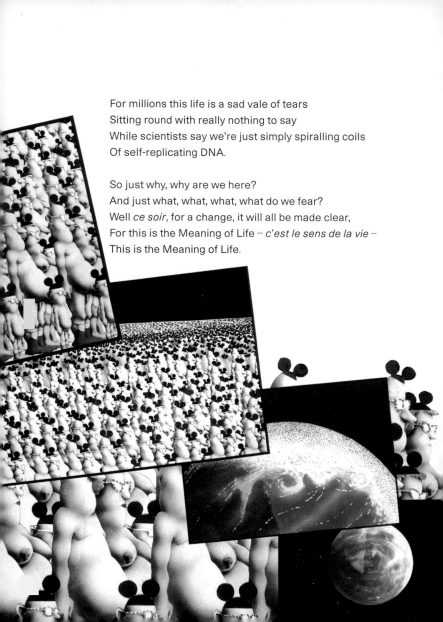

For millions this life is a sad vale of tears
Sitting round with really nothing to say
While scientists say we're just simply spiralling coils
Of self-replicating DNA.

So just why, why are we here?
And just what, what, what, what do we fear?
Well *ce soir*, for a change, it will all be made clear,
For this is the Meaning of Life – *c'est le sens de la vie* –
This is the Meaning of Life.

DAMMIT!
DAMMIT!!
DAMMIT.

CAREERS ADVICE FOR
MR ANCHOVY

MR ANCHOVY *is standing waiting beside a* COUNSELLOR *sitting at a desk.*

COUNSELLOR: Ah Mr Anchovy. Do sit down.

ANCHOVY: Thank you. Take the weight off the feet, eh?

COUNSELLOR: Yes, yes.

ANCHOVY: Lovely weather for the time of year, I must say.

COUNSELLOR: Enough of this gay banter. And now Mr Anchovy, you asked us to advise you which job in life you were best suited for.

ANCHOVY: That is correct, yes.

COUNSELLOR: Well I now have the results here of the interviews and the aptitude tests that you took last week, and from them we've built up a pretty clear picture of the sort of person that you are. And I think I can say, without fear of contradiction, that the ideal job for you is chartered accountancy.

ANCHOVY: But I *am* a chartered accountant.

COUNSELLOR: Jolly good. Well back to the office with you then.

ANCHOVY: No! No! No! You don't understand. I've been a chartered

accountant for the last twenty years. I want a new job. Something *exciting* that will let me *live*.

COUNSELLOR: Well chartered accountancy is rather exciting isn't it?

ANCHOVY: Exciting? No it's *not*. It's dull. Dull. *Dull*. My God it's dull, it's so desperately dull and tedious and stuffy and boring and des-per-ate-ly DULL.

COUNSELLOR: Well, er, yes Mr Anchovy, but you see your report here says that you are an extremely dull person. You see, our experts describe you as an appallingly dull fellow, unimaginative, timid, lacking in initiative, spineless, easily dominated, no sense of humour, tedious company and irrepressibly drab and awful. And whereas in most professions these would be considerable drawbacks, in chartered accountancy they are a positive boon.

ANCHOVY: But don't you see, I came here to find a new job, a new life, a new *meaning* to my existence. Can't you help me?

COUNSELLOR: Well, do you have any idea of what you want to do?

ANCHOVY: Yes, yes I have.

COUNSELLOR: What?

ANCHOVY *(boldly)*: Lion taming.

COUNSELLOR: Well yes. Yes. Of course, it's a bit of a jump isn't it? I mean, er, chartered accountancy to lion taming in one go. You don't think it might be better if you worked your way *towards* lion taming, say, via banking . . .

ANCHOVY: No, no, no, no. No. I don't want to wait. At nine o'clock tomorrow I want to be in there, taming.

COUNSELLOR: Fine, fine. But do you, do you have any qualifications?

ANCHOVY: Yes, I've got a hat.

COUNSELLOR: A hat?

ANCHOVY: Yes, a hat. A lion taming hat. A hat with 'lion tamer' on it. I got it at Harrods. And it lights up saying 'lion tamer' in great big neon letters, so that you can tame them after dark when they're less stroppy.

COUNSELLOR: I see, I see.

ANCHOVY: And you can switch it off during the day time, and claim reasonable wear and tear as allowable professional expenses under paragraph 335C . . .

COUNSELLOR: Yes, yes, yes, I do follow, Mr Anchovy, but you see the snag is . . . if I now call Mr Chipperfield and say to him, 'look here, I've got a forty-five-year-old chartered accountant with me who wants to become a lion tamer', his first question is not going to be 'does he have his own hat?' He's going to ask what sort of experience you've had with lions.

ANCHOVY: Well I . . . I've seen them at the zoo.

COUNSELLOR: Good, good, good.

ANCHOVY: Little brown furry things with short stumpy legs and great long noses. I don't know what all the fuss is about, I could tame one of those. They look pretty tame to start with.

COUNSELLOR: And these, er, these lions . . . how high are they?

ANCHOVY *(indicating a height of one foot)*: Well they're about so high, you know. They don't frighten me at all.

COUNSELLOR: Really. And do these lions eat ants?

ANCHOVY: Yes, that's right.

COUNSELLOR: Er, well, Mr Anchovy . . . I'm afraid what you've got hold of there is an anteater.

ANCHOVY: A what?

COUNSELLOR: An anteater. Not a lion. You see a lion is a huge savage beast, about five feet high, ten feet long, weighing about four

hundred pounds, running at forty miles per hour, with masses of sharp pointed teeth and nasty long razor-sharp claws that can rip your belly open before you can say 'Eric Robinson', and they look like this.

The counsellor produces large picture of a lion and shows it to Mr Anchovy who screams and passes out. He then sits up with a start.

COUNSELLOR: Now, shall I call Mr Chipperfield?

ANCHOVY: Er, no, no, no. I think your idea of making the transition to lion taming via easy stages, say via insurance . . .

COUNSELLOR: Or banking.

ANCHOVY: Or banking, yes, yes, banking that's a man's life, isn't it? Banking, travel, excitement, adventure, thrills, decisions affecting people's lives.

COUNSELLOR: Jolly good, well, er, shall I put you in touch with a bank?

ANCHOVY: Yes.

COUNSELLOR: Fine.

ANCHOVY: Er . . . no, no, no. Look, er, it's a big decision, I'd like a couple of weeks to think about it . . . er . . . you know, don't want to jump into it too quickly. Maybe three weeks. I could let you know definitely then, I just don't want to make this definite decision. I'm, er . . . *(He continues muttering nervously to himself)*

COUNSELLOR: Well this is just one of the all too many cases on our books of chartered accountancy. The only way that we can fight this terrible debilitating social disease, is by informing the general public of its consequences, by showing young people that it's just not worth it. So, so please . . . give generously . . . to this address: The League for Fighting Chartered Accountancy, 55 Lincoln House, Basil Street, London, SW3.

END

BRIAN IN
GAOL

BRIAN *wakes up with a smile on his face to find himself being dragged along a cell corridor by* TWO GUARDS. *The horrible figure of the* JAILER *spits at him and flings him into a dark damp cell, slamming the iron grate behind him and turning the key hollowly in the lock.* BRIAN *slumps to the floor. A voice comes out of the darkness behind him.*

BEN: You *lucky* bastard!

BRIAN *spins round and peers into the gloom.*

BRIAN: Who's that?

In the darkness BRIAN *just makes out an emaciated figure, suspended on the wall, with his feet off the ground, by chains round his wrists. This is* BEN.

BEN: You lucky, lucky bastard.

BRIAN: What?

BEN *(with great bitterness)*: Proper little gaoler's pet, aren't we?

BRIAN *(ruffled)*: What do you mean?

BEN: You must have slipped him a few shekels, eh!

BRIAN: Slipped him a few shekels! You saw him spit in my face!

BEN: Ohhh! What wouldn't I give to be spat at in the face! I sometimes hang awake at nights dreaming of being spat at in the face.

BRIAN: Well, it's not exactly friendly, is it? They had me in manacles.

BEN: Manacles! Oooh. *(His eyes go quite dreamy)* My idea of heaven is to be allowed to be put in manacles . . . just for a few hours. They must think the sun shines out of your arse, sonny!

BRIAN: Listen! They beat me up before they threw me in here.

BEN: Oh yeah? The only day they don't beat me up is on my birthday.

BRIAN: Oh shut up.

BEN: Well, your type makes me sick! You come in here, you get treated like Royalty, and everyone outside thinks you're a bloody martyr.

BRIAN: Oh, lay off me . . . I've had a hard time!

BEN: *You've* had a hard time! Listen, sonny! I've been here five years and they only hung me the right way up yesterday!

BRIAN: All right! All right!

BEN: I just wish I had half your luck. They must think you're Lord God Almighty!

BRIAN: What'll they do to me?

BEN: Oh, you'll probably get away with crucifixion.

BRIAN: Crucifixion!

BEN: Yeah, first offence.

BRIAN: Get away with crucifixion!

BEN: Best thing the Romans ever did for us.

BRIAN *(incredulous)*: What?

BEN: Oh yeah. If we didn't have crucifixion this country would be in a right bloody mess I tell you.

BRIAN *(who can stand it no longer)*: Guard!

BEN: Nail 'em up I say!

BRIAN *(dragging himself over to the door)*: Guard!

BEN: Nail some sense into them!

GUARD *(looking through the bars)*: What do you want?

BRIAN: I want to be moved to another cell.

The GUARD *spits in his face.*

BRIAN: Oh! *(he recoils in helpless disgust)*

BEN: Oh . . . look at that! Bloody favouritism!

GUARD: Shut up, you!

BEN: Sorry! Sorry! *(He lowers his voice)* Now take my case. I've been here five years, and every night they take me down for ten minutes, then they hang me up again . . . which I regard as very fair . . . in view of what I done and if nothing else, it's taught me to respect the Romans, it's taught me that you'll never get anywhere in life unless you're prepared to do a fair day's work for a fair day's pay.

BRIAN: Oh . . . Shut up!

At that moment a CENTURION *and* TWO GUARDS *enter.*

CENTURION: Pilate wants to see you.

BRIAN: Me?

CENTURION: Come on.

BRIAN *struggles to his feet.*

BRIAN: Pilate? What does he want to see me for?

CENTURION: I think he wants to know which way up you want to be crucified.

He laughs. The TWO SOLDIERS *smirk.* BEN *laughs uproariously.*

BEN: . . . Nice one, centurion. Like it, like it.

24

WHAT TO DO ON MEETING
The Royal Family

This depends largely on where you meet the Royal Family. If you meet the Royal Family in a surgical supply shop, it is best not to acknowledge them *at all*, as this will only lead to embarrassment on your part, and on the part of the Royal person or persons.* However, should you meet a member of the Royal Family in normal circumstances the etiquette is clear and simple. If you are wearing a hat or turban, remove it instantly, and hold it in your *left* hand, leaving your right hand free should the Royal Personage decide on manual contact. Going down on one knee would be very much appreciated, but in a crowded supermarket or shopping precinct this could cause a great deal of congestion and end up with you getting kicked over.

NEVER touch the Royal Family under any circumstances, unless you yourself have been touched by them – and even then keep your hands well above the waist.

The correct way to address the Royal Family is 'Your Majesty' or 'Your Highness', and not 'Hello Graham'.

NEVER ask the Royal Family a direct question.

For instance, should you wish to ask Princess Marina where the swimming baths are, you must say: 'The swimming baths are near here', and hope that she will say: 'No, I think you're wrong, they're over half a mile away down Thorpe Road and turn right at Hepworth's' or: 'Yes, they are near here. There they are.'

NEVER shout abuse or push or jostle the Royal Family, unless they attack *you*.

*The same applies in garages, betting shops, cinema clubs and public toilets.

THE PIRANHA BROTHERS

PULES: I walked out with Dinsdale Piranha on many occasions, and found him a charming and erudite companion. He was wont to introduce one to eminent celebrities, celebrated American singers, members of the aristocracy and other gang leaders, who he had met through his work for charities. He took a warm interest in Boys' Clubs, Sailors' Homes, Choristers' Associations and the Grenadier Guards. Mind you, there was nothing unusual about him. I should say not. Except, that Dinsdale was convinced that he was being watched by a giant hedgehog whom he referred to as 'Spiny Norman'. Normally Spiny Norman was wont to be about twelve feet from snout to tail, but when Dinsdale was depressed Norman could be anything up to eight hundred yards long. When Norman was about Dinsdale would go very quiet and start wobbling and his nose would swell up and his teeth would move about and he'd get very violent and claim that he'd laid Stanley Baldwin.

INTERVIEWER: Did it worry you that he, for example, stitched people's legs together?

PULES: Well it's better than bottling it up isn't it. He was a gentleman, Dinsdale, and what's more he knew how to treat a female impersonator.

INTERVIEWER: Most of the strange tales concern Dinsdale but what of Doug? One man who met him was Luigi Vercotti.

VERCOTTI: I had been running a successful escort agency – high class, no really, high class girls . . . we didn't have any of *that* – that was right out. So I decided to open a high class night club for the gentry at Biggleswade with International cuisine and cooking and top line acts, and not a cheap clip joint for picking up tarts . . . that was right out, I deny that completely, and one evening in walks Dinsdale with a couple of big lads, one of whom was carrying a tactical nuclear missile. They said I had bought one of their fruit machines and would I pay for it? They wanted three quarters of a million pounds.

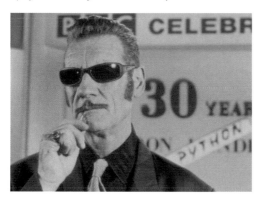

I thought about it and I decided not to go to the Police as I had noticed that the lad with the thermonuclear device was the chief constable for the area. So a week later they called again and told me the cheque had bounced and said . . . I had to see . . . Doug.

Well, I was terrified. Everyone was terrified of Doug. I've seen grown men pull their own heads off rather than see Doug. Even Dinsdale was frightened of Doug. He used . . . sarcasm. He knew all the tricks, dramatic irony, metaphor, bathos, puns, parody, litotes and . . . satire. He was vicious.

INTERVIEWER: In this way, by a combination of violence and sarcasm, the Piranha brothers by February 1966 controlled London and the South East of England. It was in February, though, that Dinsdale made a big mistake. Latterly Dinsdale had become increasingly worried about Spiny Norman. He had come to the conclusion that Norman slept in an aeroplane hangar at Luton Airport. And so on Feb 22nd 1966, Dinsdale blew up Luton.

Well, hello and welcome to page twenty nine. In many books, page 29 is a sad anti-climax after the exciting events described on pages 27 and 28. We hope to avoid this pitfall by making our page 29 into one of the most exciting and action-packed page 29s that you've ever read. In a lot of books, page 29 contains purely descriptive matter, and in others it is still only part of the introduction, but not so this one. . . . We say: get a move on, novelists! and let's have more page 29s like this one.

of her dress as it rode up over her thighs, her slender body thrust forward by the enormous power of the 6,000h.p. engines, as Horst hurled the car into a shrieking, sickening slide across the wet tarmac. The lion tore savagely at his bronzed thighs as the car soared into the air, turned, twisted, and plunged down the treacherous ski slope, that no man had ever survived. Tenderly Eunice caressed him as the fighters screeched out of the darkness, flames ripping towards him. The sea was coming nearer and nearer, and though neither had eaten for eight weeks, the stark terror of what they saw, gave them the last drop of energy to push their bodies to the limits. Eunice groaned, the dark figure of Shahn-el-Shid, dagger raised, hurled himself from the sheer wall of the palace. Horst reversed, swerved, coughed and threw himself into the gorge. Never had Horst known such exquisite pleasure, as far above him a million Dervishes swept into the fort, looting and pillaging. The Colonel screamed an order, and with one enormous blast the refinery was a sheet of flame — a wall of fire six miles long and eight miles high. Eunice groaned as the spacecraft roared low over the silent, darkened surface of this eerie world, a million light years from the Earth they had left only seconds before, a planet doomed to extinction, when suddenly

29

How about that for a page 29 ? Wake up Dickens! Wake up Graham Greene! Let's show the world that British literature gets on with it!

THE GERMAN
LUMBERJACK SONG

Ich bin ein Holzfäller und fühl mich stark
Ich schlaf des Nachts und hack am Tag.

CHORUS: Er ist ein Holzfäller und fühlt sich stark
Er schläft des Nachts und hackt am Tag.

Ich fälle Bäume, ich ess mein Brot
Ich geh auf das WC.
Am Mittwoch geh ich shopping
Kau Kekse zum Kaffee.

CHORUS: Er fällt die Bäume, er isst sein Brot
Er geht auf das WC.
Am Mittwoch geht er shopping
Kaut Kekse zum Kaffee.
Er ist ein Holzfäller und fühlt sich stark
Er schläft des Nachts und hackt am Tag.

Ich fälle Bäume und hupf und spring
Steck Blumen in die Vas.
Ich schlupf in Frauenkleider
Und lummel mich in Bars.

CHORUS: Er fällt Bäume, er hupft und springt
Steckt Blumen in die Vas.
Er schlupft in Frauenkleider

30

Und lummelt sich in Bars . . .?
Er ist ein Holzfäller und fühlt sich stark
Er schläft des Nachts und hackt am Tag.

Ich fälle Bäume, trag Stockelschuh
Und Strumpf und Bustenhalter
Wär gern ein kleines Mädchen
So wie mein Onkel Walter.

CHORUS: Er fällt die Bäume, trägt Stockelschuh
Und Strumpf und Bustenhalter . . .?

WOODY WORDS &
TINNY WORDS

*An upper-class drawing room. Father, mother and daughter having
tea. Four motionless servants stand behind them.*

FATHER: I say . . .

DAUGHTER: Yes, Daddy?

FATHER: Croquet hoops look damn pretty this afternoon.

DAUGHTER: Frightfully damn pretty.

MOTHER: They're coming along awfully well this year.

FATHER: Yes, better than your Aunt Lavinia's croquet hoops.

DAUGHTER: Ugh! – dreadful tin things.

MOTHER: I did tell her to stick to wood.

FATHER: Yes, you can't beat wood . . . Gorn!

MOTHER: What's gorn, dear?

FATHER: Nothing, nothing, I just like the word. It gives me confidence.

Gorn . . . gorn. It's got a sort of woody quality about it. Gorn. Gorn.
Much better than 'newspaper' or 'litterbin'.

DAUGHTER: Frightful words.

MOTHER: Perfectly dreadful.

FATHER: Ugh! Newspaper! . . . litterbin . . . dreadful tinny sort of words.
Tin, tin, tin.

The daughter bursts into tears.

MOTHER: Oh, dear, don't say 'tin' to Rebecca, you know how it upsets
her.

FATHER *(to the daughter)*: Sorry old horse.

MOTHER: Sausage!

FATHER: Sausage . . . there's a good woody sort of word, 'sausage' . . .
gorn.

DAUGHTER: Antelope.

FATHER: Where? On the lawn? *(He picks up a rifle)*

DAUGHTER: No, no, daddy . . . just the word.

FATHER: Don't want an antelope nibbling the hoops.

DAUGHTER: No, antelope . . . sort of nice and woody type of thing.

MOTHER: Don't think so, Becky old chap.

FATHER: No, no 'antelope', 'antelope' – tinny sort of word *(The daughter
bursts into tears)* Oh! Sorry old man . . .

MOTHER: Really, Mansfield.

FATHER: Well, she's got to come to terms with these things . . . seemly .
. . prodding . . . vacuum . . . leap . . .

DAUGHTER *(miserably)*: Hate 'leap'.

MOTHER: Perfectly dreadful.

DAUGHTER: Sort of PVC-y sort of word, don't you know.

MOTHER: Lower-middle.

FATHER: Bound!

MOTHER: Now you're talking.

FATHER: Bound . . . Vole . . . Recidivist.

MOTHER: Bit tinny. *(The daughter howls)* Oh! Sorry, Becky old beast. *(The daughter runs out crying)*

FATHER: Oh dear, suppose she'll be gorn for a few days now.

MOTHER: Caribou!

FATHER: Splendid word.

MOTHER: No dear . . . nibbling the hoops.

FATHER *(he fires a shot)*: Caribou gorn.

MOTHER *(laughs politely)*

FATHER: Intercourse.

MOTHER: Later, dear.

FATHER: No, no, the word, 'intercourse' – good and woody . . . inter . . . course . . . pert . . . pert thighs . . . botty, botty, botty . . . *(The mother leaves the room)* . . . erogenous . . . zone . . . concubine . . . erogenous zone! Loose woman . . . erogenous zone . . .

(The mother returns and throws a bucket of water over him) Oh thank you, dear . . . you know, it's a funny thing, dear . . . all the naughty words sound woody.

MOTHER: Really, dear? . . . How about tit?

FATHER: Oh dear, I hadn't thought about that. Tit. Tit. Oh, that's very tinny isn't it? *(The daughter returns)* Ugh! Tinny, tinny . . . *(The daughter runs out crying)* Oh dear . . . ocelot . . . wasp . . . yowling . . . Oh dear, I'm bored . . . I'd better go and have a bath, I suppose.

MOTHER: Oh really, must you dear? You've had nine today.

FATHER: All right, I'll sack one of the servants . . . Simkins! . . . nasty tinny sort of name. Simkins! *(He exits)*

A pilot from the RAF banter scene* enters.

PILOT: I say, mater, cabbage crates coming over the briny.

MOTHER *(frowns and shakes her head)*: Sorry dear, don't understand.

PILOT: Er . . . cowcatchers creeping up on the conning towers . . .

MOTHER: No . . . sorry . . . old sport.

PILOT: Caribou nibbling at the croquet hoops.

MOTHER: Yes, Mansfield shot one in the antlers.

PILOT: Oh, jolly good show. Is 'Becca about?

MOTHER: No, she's gorn orff.

PILOT: What a super woody sort of phrase. 'Gorn orff'.

MOTHER: Yes, she's gorn orff because Mansfield said 'tin' to her.

PILOT: Oh, what rotten luck . . . oh well . . . whole afternoon to kill . . . better have a bath I suppose.

MOTHER: Oh, Gervaise do sing me a song . . .

PILOT: Oh, OK.

MOTHER: Something woody.

The pilot launches into a quite enormously loud rendering of 'She's going to marry Yum Yum'. The impact of this on the MOTHER *causes her to have a heart attack. She dies and the song ends.*

PILOT: For . . . she's going to marry Yum Yum . . . oh crikey. The old song finished her orff.

FATHER *(entering)*: What's urp?

PILOT: I'm afraid Mrs Vermin Jones appears to have passed orn.

FATHER: Dead, is she?

PILOT: 'Fraid so.

FATHER: What a blow for her.

THE OLD
STORYTELLER

Hello boys and girls. I'm the old storyteller. Today I'd like to tell you about an amazing land in a far, far off place, where no one ever has the wobbles. In this fabulous land even the clouds are free to go where they please.

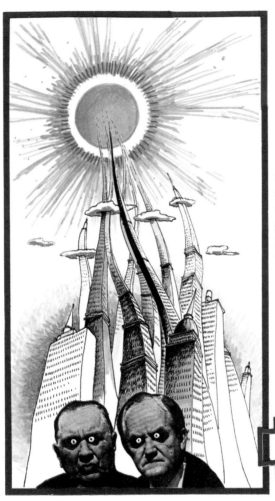

On Sundays they can go in small, well-chaperoned groups to the vast plasterboard cities that pierce the sun.

Near these cities grow shining black mountains. And near these mountains live bulging purple seas full of fishes of every known race, creed, and/or colour.

41

High above the water stand strange birds whose feet never quite reach the ground.

And on their wings live small brown roundish things that have amazed and astounded the crowned heads of Europe for over 300 years.

a crowned head   amazed   astounded

The birds are not the only things that don't touch the ground in this strange land. Unfortunately the topsoil is very light, too light in fact to stay in contact with the ground and so it floats 3 feet above it.

This would not be so bad, but for the fact that the people of this land do everything by fours, including walking on them.

And so, most of the people choose to live in the vast plasterboard cities where topsoil is not allowed - except a bit on Thursdays and on another day they don't have a name for. As I said, I would like to tell you about this amazing land, but the bastards who put this book together have only given me six pages and insist I finish so they can get on with the pretentious so-called funny stuff they've prepared. If I was younger and still had my health they wouldn't dare treat me like this. I'd have my own book. But there you go just because I smell funny and can't make it to the toilet in time. PUNKS.

STAN'S RIGHT TO
HAVE BABIES

A Roman amphitheatre. The REVOLUTIONARIES – REG, FRANCIS, STAN *and* JUDITH, *are seated in the stands. They speak conspiratorially.*

JUDITH: . . . Any Anti-Imperialist group like ours must *reflect* such a divergence of interests within its power-base.

REG: Agreed.

General nodding.

Francis?

FRANCIS: I think Judith's point of view is valid here, Reg, provided the Movement never forgets that it is the inalienable right of every man . . .

STAN: Or woman.

FRANCIS: Or woman . . . to rid himself . . .

STAN: Or herself.

REG: Or herself. Agreed. Thank you, brother.

STAN: Or sister.

FRANCIS: Thank you, brother. Or sister. Where was I?

REG: I thought you'd finished.

FRANCIS: Oh did I? Right.

REG: Furthermore, it is the birthright of every man . . .

STAN: Or woman.

REG: Why don't you shut up about women, Stan, you're putting us off.

STAN: Women have a perfect right to play a part in our movement, Reg.

FRANCIS: Why are you always on about women, Stan?

STAN: . . . I want to be one.

REG: . . . What?

STAN: I want to be a woman. From now on I want you all to call me Loretta.

REG: What!?

STAN: It's my right as a man.

JUDITH: Why do you want to be Loretta, Stan?

STAN: I want to have babies.

REG: You want to have babies????!!!

STAN: It's every man's right to have babies if he wants them.

REG: But you can't have babies.

STAN: Don't you oppress me.

REG: I'm not oppressing you. Stan – you haven't got a womb. Where's the foetus going to gestate? You going to keep it in a box?

STAN *starts crying.*

JUDITH: Here! I've got an idea. Suppose you agree that he can't actually have babies, not having a womb, which is nobody's fault, not even the Romans', but that he can have the *right* to have babies.

FRANCIS: Good idea, Judith. We shall fight the oppressors for your right to have babies, brother. Sister, sorry.

46

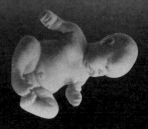

REG: What's the point?

FRANCIS: What?

REG: What's the point of fighting for his right to have babies, when he can't have babies?

FRANCIS: It is symbolic of our struggle against oppression.

REG: It's symbolic of his struggle against reality.

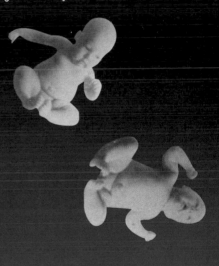

47

SEXCRAFT

THE VIBRA-PHONE:

GPO permission needed Contact your friends at intimate moments. Let them hear *how* you miss them. Dial TIM, or the weather forecast. Dial LONDON TOURIST INFORMATION, or The Latest Test Score without interrupting your private life.

VIBRADIO:

Current Radio Licence required in the British Isles. *Why Miss Your Favourites?* Listen to the Archers as never before. Contribute to 'Any Answers' without leaving the comfort of your own bed (or somebody else's).

VHF:

Car Model Also Available, Plugs in the Mains. Just watch it go. Lasts a whole weekend without any messy battery changes.

THE 'THOMPSON' WALLET SUPPORTER:

For the maturer man who finds his freedom of movement restricted by the size of his wallet. The 'THOMPSON' Wallet Supporter gives uplift in 3 vital areas: (a) credit cards (b) huge wads of fivers and (c) freds. With the 'THOMPSON' Wallet Supporter even the most successful businessman can jump and roll around unfettered.

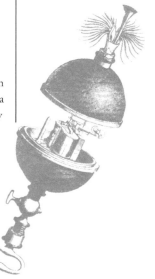

THE 'ALADDIN':

No more tiresome ejaculations! The 'ALADDIN' produces a realistic squeal, as of a pig being trodden on, at the crucial moment, thereby distracting your partner's attention, and providing YOU with an alibi.

THE 'WIDGERY' BLACKMAIL NOTE:

A really safe document. (Guaranteed untraceable – contains no ex-works no. or address) Simply fill in the amount required, the name of the blackmailee, the place to leave the money, and some rough indication of the sexual practice to be revealed, in the spaces provided on the note, and 'hey-presto!' you're rich overnight!

THE 'GROSVENOR' ARM CHAIR:

A real post-coital 'must' for all active people. After a good bang, sit down and relax in the 'Grosvenor' Range of Furniture. 'A really comfortable armchair' *The Sun* ('Grosvenor' Post-Coital Products, Brighton)

SHEATHS etc.

THE OMAR SHEATH:
Uncircumcised
rubberware

THE WHOOPEE-SHEATH:
Makes a rude noise when sat on.
Startle your friends.

THE 'WHAT'S THAT SONNY?':
For the smaller man.

THE PROTECTORS:
Thursdays. Television Series. ATV

THE PATRIOT'S PROTECTOR:
Available in red, white and blue.
Also:
Stars and Stripes
Union Jack
Tricolour
Hammer and Sickle
Maple Leaf

JOINT:
This one's for passing around.

THE BOSTON STARTLER:
Available for the larger gentleman.
In several colours: black, brown and
Australian.

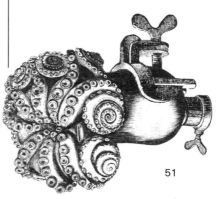

WHY ACCOUNTANCY
IS NOT BORING

Why accountancy is not boring by Mr A. Putey

First let me say how very pleased I was to be asked on the 14th inst. to write an article on why accountancy is not boring. I feel very very strongly that there are many people who may think that accountancy *is* boring, but they would be wrong, for it is not at all boring, as I hope to show you in this article, which is, as I intimated earlier, a pleasure to write.

I think I can do little worse than begin this article by describing why accountancy is *not* boring as far as *I* am concerned, and then, perhaps, go on to a more general discussion of why accountancy as a whole is not boring. As soon as I awake in the morning it is not boring. I get up at 7.16, and my wife Irene, an ex-schoolteacher, gets up shortly afterwards at 7.22. Breakfast is far from boring, and soon I am ready to leave the house. Irene, a keen Rotarian, hands me my briefcase and rolled umbrella at 7.53, and I leave the house seconds later. It is a short walk to Sutton station, but by no means a boring one. There is so much to see, including Mr Edgeworth, who also works at Robinson Partners. Mr Edgeworth is an extremely interesting man, and was in Uxbridge during the war. I think that many of the people to whom accountancy appears boring think that all accountants are the same. Nothing could be further from the truth. Some accountants are chartered, but very many others are certified. I am a certified accountant, as indeed is Mr Edgeworth, whom I told you about earlier. However, in the next office to mine is a Mr Manners, who is a chartered accountant, and, incidentally, a keen Rotarian. So far, as you can see, accountancy is not boring. During the morning there are a hundred and one things to do. A secretary may pop in with details of an urgent audit. This happened in 1967 and again last year. On the other hand, the phone may ring, or there may be details of a new superannuation scheme to mull over. The time flies by in this not at all boring way, and it is soon 10.00, when there is only 1 hour to go before Mrs Jackson brings round the tea urn. At 11.05, having drunk an interesting cup of tea, I put my cup on the tray and then . . .

(18 *pages deleted here* – Ed.) . . . and once the light is turned out by Irene, a very keen Rotarian, I am left to think about how extremely un-boring my day has been, being an accountant. Finally may I say how extremely grateful I am to your book for so generously allowing me so much space. (*Sorry, Putey!* – Ed.)

53

THE PRINCE
IN THE TOWER

A young, quite embarrassingly unattractive PRINCE *is gazing out of a castle window. His* FATHER *stands beside him. He is also looking out.*

FATHER: One day lad, all this will be yours . . .

PRINCE: What – the curtains?

FATHER: No! Not the curtains, lad . . . all that . . . *(he indicates the vista from the window)* all that you can see, stretched out over the hills and valleys . . . as far as the eye can see and beyond . . . that'll be your kingdom, lad.

PRINCE: But, Mother . . .

FATHER: Father, lad.

PRINCE: But, Father, I don't want any of that, I'd rather . . .

FATHER: Rather what?

PRINCE: I'd rather . . . just . . . sing . . .

Music starts.

FATHER: You're not going into a song while I'm here!

Music stops.

Listen, lad, in twenty minutes you're going to be married to a girl whose father owns the biggest tracts of open land in Britain . . .

PRINCE: I don't want land.

FATHER: Listen, Alice . . .

PRINCE: Herbert.

FATHER: Herbert . . . You're marrying Princess Lucky, so you'd better get used to the idea! Guards!

TWO GUARDS *enter and stand to attention on either side of the door. One of them has hiccoughs.*

FATHER: Make sure the Prince doesn't leave this room until I come and get him.

FIRST GUARD: Not . . . to leave the room . . . even if you come and get him.

FATHER: No. *Until* I come and get him.

SECOND GUARD: Hic.

FIRST GUARD: Until you come and get him, we're not to enter the room.

FATHER: No . . . You stay in the room and make sure he doesn't leave.

FIRST GUARD: . . . and you'll come and get him.

SECOND GUARD: Hic.

FATHER: That's right.

FIRST GUARD: We don't need to do anything apart from just stop him entering the room.

FATHER: Leaving the room.

FIRST GUARD: Leaving the room . . .yes.

FATHER: Got it?

SECOND GUARD: Hic.

FIRST GUARD: Er . . . if . . . we . . . er . . .

FATHER: Yes?

55

FIRST GUARD: If we . . . er . . . *(trying to remember what he was going to say)*

FATHER: Look, it's simple. Just stay here and make sure he doesn't leave the room.

SECOND GUARD: Hic.

FATHER: Right?

FIRST GUARD: Oh, I remember . . . can he . . . er . . . can he leave the room *with* us?

FATHER *(carefully)*: No . . . keep him in here . . . and make sure he doesn't . . .

FIRST GUARD: Oh, yes! We'll keep him in here, obviously. But if he *had* to leave . . . and we were with him.

FATHER: No . . . just keep him in here.

FIRST GUARD: Until you, or anyone else . . .

FATHER: No. Not anyone else – just me.

FIRST GUARD: Just you . . .

SECOND GUARD: Hic.

FIRST GUARD: Get back.

FATHER: Right.

FIRST GUARD: Okay. Fine. We'll remain here until you get back.

FATHER: And make sure he doesn't leave.

FIRST GUARD: What?

FATHER: Make sure he doesn't leave.

FIRST GUARD: The Prince . . .?

FATHER: Yes . . . make sure . . .

FIRST GUARD: Oh yes, of course! I thought you meant *him*!

(He points to the other GUARD and laughs to himself.) . . . you know, it seemed a bit daft me having to guard him when he's a guard . . .

FATHER: Is that clear?

SECOND GUARD: Hic.

FIRST GUARD: Oh, yes. That's quite clear. No problem.

FATHER *pulls open the door and makes to leave the room. The* GUARDS *follow.*

FATHER *(to the* GUARDS*)*: Where are you going?

FIRST GUARD: We're coming with you.

FATHER: No, I want you to stay here and make sure he doesn't leave the room until I get back.

FIRST GUARD: Oh, I see, right.

They take up positions on either side of the door.

PRINCE: But, Father.

FATHER: Shut your noise, you, and get that suit on!

He points to a wedding suit on a chair. FATHER *throws one last look at the* PRINCE *and turns, goes out and slams the door.*

The PRINCE *slumps on to a window seat, looking forlornly out of the window. . . .*

Music starts . . .

The door flies open, the music cuts off and FATHER *pokes his head in.*

FATHER: And NO SINGING!

SECOND GUARD: Hic.

FATHER *(as he goes out)*: Go and have a drink of water.

58

I'm so worried about what's happening today
In the Middle East, you know
And I'm so worried about the baggage retrieval
System they've got at Heathrow.

I'm so worried about the fashions today
I don't think they're good for your feet
And I'm so worried about the shows on TV
That sometimes they want to repeat.

I'm so worried about what's happening today, you know
And I'm worried about the baggage retrieval
System they've got at Heathrow . . .

I'm so worried about modern technology
I'm so worried about all the things that they dump in the sea
I'm so worried about it, worried about it,
Worried, worried, worried . . .

I'm so worried about everything that can go wrong
I'm so worried about whether people like this song
I'm so worried about this very next verse
It isn't the best that I've got
And I'm so worried about whether I should go on
Or whether I shouldn't just stop.

PUBLISHER'S WARNING

Page 59 is missing, believed to be held captive by a breakaway group of terrorists loyal to page 29. They have threatened to cut off a piece of the page and send it back to the publishers every day until their demands are met.

d.
ev.
still
done
forev.

I'm worried about whether I ought to have stopped
And I'm worried because it's the sort of thing I ought to know
And I'm so worried about the baggage retrieval
System they've got at Heathrow.

I'm so worried about whether I should have stopped then
I'm so worried that I'm driving everyone round the bend
I'm worried about the baggage retrieval
System they've got at Heathrow.

We WARNeD YOU!

...hing a limp thoroughl...
...nd placing the tongue in b...
...thereby creating £10,000,0...
...ich and prosperous with me...

59

A PREFACE BY
ERIC IDLE
FOR PEOPLE WHO HAVE MISTAKENLY OPENED THIS BOOK UPSIDE DOWN AND BACK TO FRONT... AND ON PAGE 66 (NOT 99)

I cannot believe these people are seriously trying to rip you off once again by banging out selected passages from old Python books. I mean have they no shame? It's not like this stuff was any good the first time around, but to reprint it and shovel it out once more, well whatever is next? Python in Urdu? Ancient Flying Circus skits in Braille? The Best of the Finest Reprinted Sketches hand tinted and printed backwards for your reading pleasure? Maybe they'll broaden the concept – Michael Palin's Best Bits of the Bible or John Cleese's Highlights from Shakespeare, or Terry Jones' favourite fictional shags.

This one is apparently edited by someone called Terry Gilliam. I don't remember him, but one of my scantily-clad, tiny, but perfectly formed, Philippino assistants has just come off the Internet with the interesting information that he is apparently an unemployed film director and once did the disgusting drawings for the Python shows. Oh yes now I remember him, he had long hair and rather a cute little ass .

. . I never knew he could read. And now he's *editing*? Still, it's your money, or *was* until you plonked it down for this piece of unadulterated garbage. So don't come running to me, moaning and grumbling about how you've been ripped off because I don't stand to gain one single penny . . . what? *How much?* Really? Wow. Okay.

This is one of the finest books in the world. Lovingly hand edited by the genius of Terry Gilliam this wonderful piece of work will bring you hours and hours of sheer unadulterated pleasure. I can thoroughly recommend it to everybody in the entire world.

E.I. February 2000

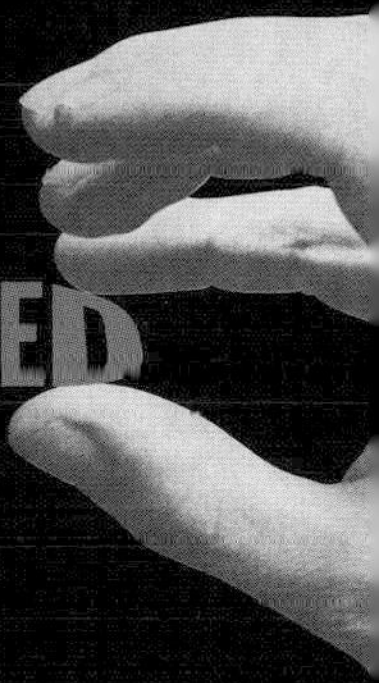

SELECTED
BY
ERIC
IDLE

WITH A PREFACE BY TERRY JONES
AND A FOREWORD BY THE LATE
GRAHAM CHAPMAN

FOR
GEORGE
AKA MR PAPADOPOULOS

WITH LOVE FROM
JOHN, MICHAEL, TERRY, ERIC
TERRY AND GRAHAM

A PREFACE BY
TERRY JONES

It is a great honour to have the privilege of writing this Preface for a book the contents of which have been selected by Eric Idol. Eric first came into my life when I was three months old. He had not been born at the time, but was able to communicate via the amniotic fluid in a simple version of morse code that he had developed. The first message I remember receiving from him informed me that, when he got out, he was expecting a Porsche. A month later he amended this and told me that if I thought a mere motor car was going to tempt him out of the womb, I had another think coming. He was, his message said, quite content to stay where he was.

Eight months later I received another communication from Eric. It was full of pain and outrage. Things, it appeared, were not going well between his mother and himself. He had a dreadful feeling that she was, in some way, 'trying to expel him', as he put it, but that he was going to do his damnedest to 'stick in there'.

The next time I heard from Eric, it was via a boiled egg that he had managed to smuggle into a shopping basket belonging to a local chiropodist that my father used. It turned out that Eric had lost his earlier struggle with his genetrix, but was now reconciled to a life outside the womb, as long as the Porsche turned up, which it hadn't done so far.

I e-mailed back to say that, while I sympathised, I thought an Aston Martin might be a more suitable compensation for having to live in the real world. This was, remarkably, the first time that e-mail had been used. But, in 1944, there was no way Eric could have picked the message up. And so it was that our correspondence dwindled to a mere trickle during the post-war era of Clement Attlee, Nye Bevan and the great egg shortage of 1944–1947.

Eric would send a trickle. I would reply with an even smaller trickle. Eric would respond with several trickles and a runny bit. I would return a big trickle and a wet patch and so on and so forth. None of it meant much to either of us, but it was a comfort to know that neither of us was the only one with a weak bladder.

The truth is that Eric has always been an innovative and original communicator – one has only to think of his attempt to send messages across the Hackney Marshes by re-arranging the drainage channels so that they spelt out the first letters of the word chloroplast, or his release of lizards into the sewage system of Manhattan, in which each lizard had tied round its neck a message to one of the Beverly Sisters.

And he has remained an extraordinary communicator to this day. Why only yesterday a huge boulder, measuring 60ft in diameter, fell off my roof – crushing me to death. On the boulder in clearly chiselled Bodoni Light was the message: 'Oops! Sorry! – love Ratty'.

I shall miss Eric and our correspondence, but, being dead, I can't get too upset about it. And besides, it is enough to know that this magnificent book – a truly worthy and delightful memorial of those Golden Days behind the bicycle sheds, when a pack of ten Weights Woodbines only cost a year's wages, and all wellington boots had holes in – is now safely in your hands.

I hope, that through the medium of this volume, Eric will continue to communicate with you in the same spiritual and essentially daffy way that he has communicated with me throughout our lives and beyond.

T. J. October 2002

ABOUT **THE EDITOR**

Eric Idle was the nicest of the six members of Monty Python. He was born in the North of England well when I say the nicest he wasn't *absolutely* the nicest. Michael Palin is generally recognized as being the nicest. Actually Terry Jones is pretty nice too, and certainly he's very nice at parties. It's probably fair to say that he is at least as nice as Michael Palin at parties. Come to think of it Terry Gilliam can be fairly nice as well. Especially abroad. In fact he is super nice abroad. Perhaps almost too nice. That Graham Chapman was a nice man and even John Cleese is a lot nicer than he used to be. In fact I'd stick my neck out and say that nowadays John Cleese is probably amongst the nicest of them all. So, Eric Idle is the *sixth* nicest member of the old Monty Python group. He was born in the North of England, what's so great about being nice anyway? Many fine people have lived richly fulfilling lives without having to worry about being nice. Nobody said Mozart was 'nice'. They didn't say 'I loved Shakespeare's *Hamlet* but what a nice guy he is.' In fact many great artists weren't very nice at all. So let's just agree to leave the nice thing to one side. Eric Idle, while not being necessarily the nicest of the Monty Python group was born in the North of England during World War Two. He went to a not particularly nice boarding school in Wolverhampton from the age of seven. That's not going to make anyone very nice is it? He attended Nice College, Cambridge, oh all right *Pembroke* College, Cambridge, and became President of the Footlights (just like Peter Cook and no one ever accused *him* of being nice did they? He'd have laughed in their faces if they had. 'Don't you call me nice you daft old git' he'd have said, in that funny voice, and he'd have been absolutely right).

Eric Idle was born in the North of England and etc etc Cambridge. During the sixties and early seventies he was occasionally mistaken for Peter Cook. He now lives in California and is occasionally mistaken for Gene Wilder. He is still not particularly nice.

HOW TO TALK TO
THE QUEEN

A typical conversation with The Queen

QUEEN: Arise.

ORDINARY MAN: Thank you, your Majesty.

QUEEN: What brings you to Wolverhampton?

ORDINARY MAN: I have an aunt who lives near here – well in Wellington, actually, which is just about – (*you will have lost The Queen's attention by now. She meets many people, so keep your sentences short and sharp*).

QUEEN: Well, I must be going away . . .

ORDINARY MAN: Goodbye, your Majesty.

QUEEN: Goodbye, my man.

A bad conversation with The Queen

ORDINARY MAN: Hello, I didn't recognize you.

QUEEN: But I am The Queen!

ORDINARY MAN: You don't look at all like you do on the stamps.

QUEEN: Don't you speak to me like that, you dirty little nonentity.

ORDINARY MAN: Can you help me change this wheel?

QUEEN: Shut your fat gob, you nasty little pile of wombat's do's.

A conversation like this could ruin your chances of an O.B.E.

THE BATLEY LADIES
TOWNSWOMEN'S GUILD

President: Mrs Rita Fairbanks
Mrs Fairbanks reports on this year's production

This has been a terribly good year for the Guild. Our annual production raised more than ever and was even more popular. Thanks are due to Mrs Lowndes for doing the cakes, and of course the Vicar for the use of the field. We were the first Townswomen's Guild to put on 'Camp on Blood Island' and last year we did our extremely popular re-enactment of 'Nazi War Atrocities', so this year we decided to do something in a lighter vein. Happily we fell on 'The Battle of Pearl Harbor'. To all involved many thanks and let's hope that next year's production of 'Groupie' will be even more successful. Yours Truly,

Rita Fairbanks

Mrs Rita Fairbanks
The Dimples,
Bottomleigh,
Wainscotting,
Nr. Batley.

Mrs Rita Fairbanks and friends during rehearsals

Some previous productions
by the Batley Ladies Townswomen's Guild

1992 The Merchant of Venice

1993 Fiddler on the Roof

1994 Iolanthe

1995 Hair

1996 Salad Days

1997 Man of La Mancha

1998 Little Women

1999 Annie

2000 The Producers

2001 The Battle of Pearl Harbor

Children's Page

Hello children hello. This is Uncle Dennis welcoming you to your own page. Hello. Today we are going to have a story, so sit comfortably and we can all start.

One day, Rikki the magic Pixie, went to visit Daisy Bumble in her tumbledown cottage. He found her in the bedroom. Roughly he grabbed her heaving shoulders pulling her down on to the bed and hurriedly ripping off her thin ███████████████████.

Old Nick, the Sea Captain was a rough tough jolly sort of fellow. He loved the life of the sea and he loved to hang out down by the pier where the men dressed as ladies ███████████ ████████████████████████████ with a melon.

Rumpletweezer ran the Dinky Tinky shop in the foot of the Magic oak tree by the wobbly dum dum tree in the shade of the magic glade down in Dingly Dell. Here he sold contraceptives, ███████████████ and various appliances ███████████ naked fun ████████████ f ████ ███████████ sh█ ███████████

80

THE STORY OF
THE GRAIL

*Doug and Bob are Metropolitan Policemen
with a difference*

Doug slips into a little cocktail frock while Bob bouffantes his hair for a night 'on duty'

Chief suspects are the Brain twins (Nikky, Vance and Denise)
who torture a Mayfair trichologist into revealing, in a tender
and emotional death scene, that his hair is not his own . . .

Meanwhile a Kent Touring XI have trapped husky Matilda Tritt on a 'sticky' near Hastings. She reveals all before enforcing the follow-on

. . . all seems to be well when suddenly, Carol, the cockney telephone sanitiser and ex-drummer for the Who, and Ronnie Medway III, tiny-brained assistant millionaire, find new love for each other in a flashback near Hastings . . .

Alas! They are trapped on the beach at Deal by Bob and Doug, disguised as the man who edited most of the Ken Russell films. Towards the end, they all kill each other and live happily ever after

SPAMELOT!

We're Knights of the Round Table
We dance whene'er we're able
We do routines and chorus scenes
With footwork impeccable
We dine well here in Camelot
We eat ham and jam and Spam a lot.

We're Knights of the Round Table
Our shows are formidable
But many times
We're given rhymes
That are quite unsingable
We're opera-mad in Camelot
We sing from the diaphragm a lot.

In war we're tough and able,
Quite indefatigable
Between our quests
We sequin vests
And impersonate Clark Gable
It's a busy life in Camelot.
SINGLE MAN: I have to push the pram a lot . . .

OH WHAT A LOVELY
DOG

Background of mouth organ and bombs falling.

OFFICER: Home on leave in two days, eh, Sarge?

SERGEANT: Yes sir.

OFFICER: Lucky man.

SERGEANT: Oh, soon be your turn sir.

OFFICER: Yes, yes, I suppose so. Is that your wife, Sarge?

SERGEANT: Yes sir.

OFFICER: You're a lucky man.

SERGEANT: You married, sir?

OFFICER: Yes, yes, rather. Did I, er, ever show you that picture of my wife, Sarge?

SERGEANT: Well, no sir.

OFFICER: Where's the damn thing? Yes, here we are. Pretty nice, eh?

SERGEANT: Oh, bit ugly though sir.

OFFICER: Ugly?

SERGEANT: You know, I mean not attractive to men, sir.

OFFICER: Well, I suppose that's rather a matter of taste, Sarge.

SERGEANT: Oh no, no she's ugly sir.

OFFICER: It's not a very good picture actually . . . it makes her nose look too big.

SERGEANT: No, the nose is all right sir, it's the eyes.

OFFICER: What's wrong?

SERGEANT: Well they're crooked sir.

OFFICER: They're not crooked.

SERGEANT: Very crooked sir.

OFFICER: Yes, yes, I s'pose so. Is that your . . . wife Sarge?

SERGEANT: No sir, that's my dog.

OFFICER: Oh. Oh. Ah . . . good looking dog, isn't it?

SERGEANT: She sir, she's a bitch.

OFFICER: *Is* she . . . ! ?

SERGEANT: Yes sir. Oh, look out sir!

Noise of bombs.

OFFICER: Er . . . Sarge . . . ?

SERGEANT: Yes sir?

OFFICER: Er . . . this dog of yours . . . quite a little stunner, isn't she?

SERGEANT: Look out sir. Oh, do you think they're bringing up the big mortars, sir?

OFFICER: Yes. Does she, er, does she have any . . . friends . . . ?

SERGEANT: What, sir?

OFFICER: Your dog.

SERGEANT: Oh, just the other dogs in the neighbourhood sir.

OFFICER: She doesn't have a . . . er . . . steady . . . er, boyfriend?

SERGEANT: Well no sir, she's a dog.

OFFICER: Yes, yes, of course.

SERGEANT: Oh . . . blimey, it's getting bad sir.

OFFICER: Yes . . . Still, I mean, she wouldn't object to someone . . . calling on her, would she Sarge?

SERGEANT: Well I'm not sure how you mean sir.

OFFICER: Er, I mean, I was thinking, perhaps I could take her for a walk some time?

SERGEANT: Oh, yes, sir, of course sir, any time.

OFFICER: Oh thank you Sarge.

SERGEANT: Look out sir! Oooh! No, that's my wife sir.

OFFICER: Are you . . . *sure* Sarge?

SERGEANT: Yes sir, that's my wife.

OFFICER: And . . . that's your dog?

SERGEANT: Yes sir.

OFFICER: I *see* . . . Look, Sarge, I think I'll be calling on you rather a lot when all this is over.

SERGEANT: Oh, thank you sir.

OFFICER: Not at all . . . it's just that I'm . . . rather fond of dogs . . .

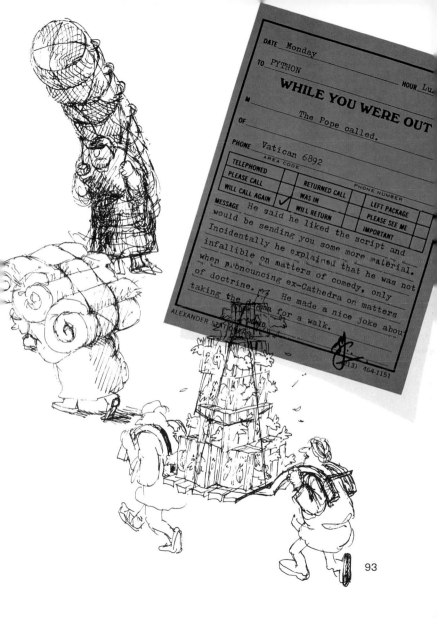

DATE Monday

TO PYTHON   HOUR Lu_

WHILE YOU WERE OUT

M _____

The Pope called.

OF _____

PHONE Vatican 6892

	AREA CODE		PHONE NUMBER
TELEPHONED			
PLEASE CALL		RETURNED CALL	
WILL CALL AGAIN	✓	WAS IN	LEFT PACKAGE
MESSAGE		WILL RETURN	PLEASE SEE ME
			IMPORTANT

MESSAGE He said he liked the script and
would be sending you some more material.
Incidentally he explained that he was not
infallible on matters of comedy, only
when pronouncing ex-Cathedra on matters
of doctrine. He made a nice joke about
taking the dogma for a walk.

ALEXANDER   (13) 464-1151

93

HOW IT ALL BEGAN–The Story of Brian

IN THE REIGN OF CAESAR AUGUSTUS THERE WENT OUT A DECREE THAT ALL THE WORLD SHOULD BE TAXED. THOUSANDS FLED INTO TAX EXILE IN JUDEA, SETTING UP OFFSHORE OVERSEAS LIMITED LIABILITY COMPANIES; AMONGST THEM, MANDY COHEN, THE MOTHER OF BRIAN, WHO WAS CARRYING THE CHILD OF NORTIUS MAXIMUS. ONE NIGHT, JUST BEFORE CHRISTMAS...

I LOVE SHEEP.

YES, SO DO I.

ME TOO. TERRIFIC ANIMALS.

NO TROUBLE.

NO, NO TROUBLE AT ALL.

EXCEPT AT SHEARING.

I LIKE THE WAY THEY GET A LITTLE BIT CROSS AT SHEARING. IT SHOWS THEY'RE HUMAN.

OH YEAH. I WASN'T SAYING I *DIS*LIKE THEM AT SHEARING, BUT THEY *CAN* BE A BIT OF A HANDFUL, CAN'T THEY?

SO WOULD *YOU* BE, IF YOU HAD A GREAT PAIR OF SCISSORS SNIPPING AWAY AT YOU WHILE SOMEBODY HELD YOUR BACK LEGS.

DON'T GET ME WRONG, MORRIS. I ACTUALLY *LOVE* SHEEP. I'D DO *ANYTHING* FOR THEM.

AND THE LITTLE LAMBS IN SPRINGTIME.

HOW IT ALL KEPT ON BEGINNING...

TOWARDS 0 B.C. EVERYONE GOT A LITTLE CRAZY BECAUSE THEY'D BEEN COUNTING THE YEARS BACKWARDS, AND THEY WERE RUNNING OUT OF NUMBERS. SO WHEN THEY GOT TO THE YEAR MINUS ONE, EVERYONE JUST KINDA FREAKED BECAUSE NOBODY WANTED TO REACH THE NUMBER 0, WHICH IS INFINITY. SO THEY SORTA COMPROMISED, AND SWITCHED RIGHT IN TO PLUS ONE, WHICH IS 1 A.D. (ONLY THE OTHER 0. DROPPED OFF).

SHHH! I HEARD SOMETHING MOVING OUT THERE.

WOLVES?

COULD BE.

RIGHT. TAKE THAT, YOU BUGGER!

OW!

WHAT DID YOU DO THAT FOR?

SORRY. WE THOUGHT YOU WERE A WOLF.

WAIT TILL YOU'VE HEARD WHAT WE'VE SEEN...! THE MOST INCREDIBLE, MIRACULOUS THING HAS JUST HAPPENED...

DON'T TELL THEM.

BUT THEY SAID WE WERE TO TELL EVERYBODY.

SOLLY & SARAH

SOLLY: What do you mean, the Holy Ghost?

SARAH: I said, the Holy Ghost done it.

SOLLY: He got you up the gut, the Holy Ghost did?

SARAH: Yeah.

SOLLY: You expect me to believe that the Holy Ghost took a night off from heaven, came down to number 42, Sheep Way, and shacked up with you.

SARAH: Yeah.

SOLLY: Let me get this right – the Spiritual Ruler of the entire Universe, feeling a touch randy and in need of a bit of the other, manifests himself, comes down and nips into bed with you.

SARAH: Yeah.

SOLLY: Nice one. I don't get a bit of nooky out of you for two years and next thing you're having knee tremblers with a bloody archangel.

SARAH: He's not a bloody archangel, he's the Holy Ghost.

SOLLY: Oh yeah – if the Holy Ghost climbs into bed with you – it's down with the sheets and on with the job. If it's me, it's no, not till after we're married, we must save it up it's precious.

SARAH: It's true.

SOLLY: It's so fucking precious you give it to every horny little poltergeist that comes banging on the bedroom door.

SARAH: Only one.

SOLLY: Oh only one. Sorry, not the Trinity. Three persons in one bed; no, just one sexy little seraph at a time. Sorry Solly I'm saving my cherry for a cherub.

SARAH: I couldn't turn him down, he's the Holy Ghost.

SOLLY: What did he look like, did he have his head tucked under his arm?

SARAH: He's not that sort of a ghost.

SOLLY: How do I know what sort of a ghost he is, I've not been to bed with the bugger. Madame Palm's all I get for two years, not you no, you've got your feet in the air, being humped by Heavenly visitors.

SARAH: It was spiritual.

SOLLY: If it was so spiritual how come he's left his little gift in you?

SARAH: It's a blessing.

SOLLY: I notice he doesn't stay around for the blessing. Oh no, far too busy dipping his holy wick in the lamps of foolish virgins. I mean I feel frankly, that if the Holy Ghost is going around shagging all and sundry the least he can do is stick around and see his offspring through the crèche stage.

SARAH: He said I was to tell you and you'd understand and marry me.

SOLLY: I see. I see. So my idea of the perfect wife is supposed to be someone who puts out for any dissipated sprite who fancies getting his end away with the scarlet women of the spiritual world.

SARAH: He *was* the Holy Ghost.

SOLLY: I don't care if he's the Holy Choir Invisible. I don't want any lecherous apparitions unsheathing their pork swords in my sheets.

SARAH: He was ever so nice. He said I could call him Brian.

SOLLY: Brian.

SARAH: Yes.

SOLLY: Brian, the Holy Ghost.

SARAH: Yes.

SOLLY: And do you recollect throughout two thousand years of scriptures the Holy Ghost ever being referred to previously as Brian.

SARAH: Erm no.

SOLLY: So it never crossed your mind that this smutty seraphim, this rampant genie with his pants round his ankles, might perhaps not be an angel of the most high in rut but some quite ordinary mortal with a gift of the gab and a penchant for banging underage briffit.

SARAH: I've never done it before.

SOLLY: I'm afraid my dear you've fallen for a very old line.

Pause

SARAH: Do you want me to show you what he did?

SOLLY: What?

SARAH: Do you want me to show you what he taught me?

SOLLY: What all the way? Bareback?

SARAH: I can't get more pregnant can I?

SOLLY: No.

SARAH: Somebody's got to be second.

SOLLY: Yeah.

SARAH: It's ever so nice.

SOLLY: All right.

SARAH: Between you and me, I never fancied him that much.

SOLLY: No?

SARAH: No, it wasn't very big.

SOLLY: That's not supposed to count.

SARAH: I know. But it helps.

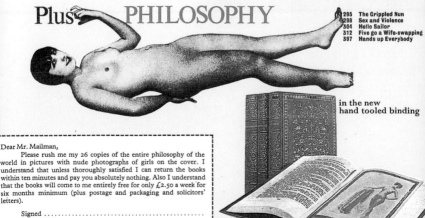

Did you know . . .

★ that El Greco's real name was E.L. Grecott?

★ Chuck Berry wrote many of Shakespeare's plays?

★ the Everly Brothers turned down a knighthood?

The Hackenthorpe Book of Lies

★ Did you know that the reason why windows steam up in cold weather is because of all the fish in the atmosphere?

★ Did you know that Moslems are forbidden to eat glass?

★ Did you know that the oldest rock in the world is the famous Hackenthorpe Rock, in North Ealing, which is 2 trillion years old?

★ Did you know that Milton was a woman?

★ Did you know that from the top of the Prudential Assurance Building in Bromley you can see 8 continents?

★ Did you know that the highest point in the world is only 8 foot?

These are just a few of the totally inaccurate facts in
THE HACKENTHORPE
BOOK OF LIES

It's all in THE HACKENTHORPE
BOOK OF LIES
A thorough and exhaustive source of
misleading and untruthful information,
compiled and edited by ex-Nobel
Prizewinners Ron Hackenthorpe, Derek
Hackenthorpe, Jeff 'The Nozz'
Hackenthorpe and Luigi V. Hackenthorpe.
There are 4 handsomely bound volumes,
which can be purchased individually, or in
our 'Pack Of Lies' gift set.

contains o
60 million
untrue fac
and figure

Some highlights from
MASTURBATORS
OF HISTORY

• 'Juste avant la grande bataille d'Austerlitz, et aussi les batailles d'Ulm et de Borodino, je m'avais preparé avec la main droite.' ('Before the great battle of Austerlitz and also the battles of Ulm and Borodino, I prepared myself with a quick one'). Napoleon (1813)

• George Washington (from his Diary July 1776): 'The struggle is over, the battle is won, today the independence for which we have given so much is ours by right and deed. I could never have done this without regularly twanging the wire.'

• Nansen (Norwegian Explorer): 'I find I explore better after punishing Percy in the palm.'

• Olof Palme (Swedish Prime Minister): No comment.

• Verdi: 'Composing operas is tough work, and I find the one sure way to relax is the man's way.'

• Leopold I (1640–1705): 'Being Holy Roman Emperor is tough work, you have enormous territories to defend, and in 1683 the Turks were at the gates of Vienna. I don't think I could have coped without some dirty books and a hanky.'

• Purcell (seventeenth-century English organist): 'One off the wrist keeps me in trim.'

• Michaelangelo: 'E parate di pristavere e dimmaggione con brio Sistine marvelloso giondore.'
('Painting the roof of the Sistine Chapel is tough work. Self-abuse keeps me going').

LAVISHLY ILLUSTRATED

Masturbators of History is an entirely new way of looking at history (writes Kenneth Onan, rather shakily). For the first time we glimpse the behind-the-scenes happenings that may have influenced the course of history: the famous cross-hand during the signing of the Treaty of Utrecht, the Papal Bull making the practice compulsory during the Thirty Years War (owing to a misprint), and the reason Pilate really washed his hands. We see how it has shaped the careers of writers, musicians (especially pianists), generals and politicians. Why did Beethoven go deaf? Why was Toulouse Lautrec so small? What did Sir Walter Raleigh do in the Tower? All this and more in this fully illustrated Historical handbook. Published by Slater-Wristjob.

THE
BRUCES PHILOSOPHERS SONG

Immanuel Kant was a real pissant
Who was very rarely stable

Heidegger, Heidegger was a boozy beggar
Who could think you under the table

David Hume could out-consume
Schopenhauer and Hegel

And Wittgenstein was a beery swine
Who was just as schloshed as Schlegel

There's nothing Nietzsche couldn't teach ya
'Bout the raising of the wrist
Socrates, himself, was permanently pissed.

John Stuart Mill, of his own free will,
On half a pint of shandy was particularly ill

Plato, they say, could stick it away
Half a crate of whisky every day

Aristotle, Aristotle was a bugger for the bottle
Hobbes was found of his dram

And René Descartes was a drunken fart
'I drink, therefore I am'.

Yes, Socrates himself is particularly missed
A lovely little thinker
But a bugger when he's pissed.

CHEZ BRUCE

1. *Black Stump Bordeaux*
A peppermint-flavoured Burgundy.
2. *Sydney Syrup*
Can rank with any of the world's best sugary wines.
3. *Châteaublue*
Has won many prizes, not least for its taste, and its lingering afterburn.
4. *Old Smokey 1968*
Compares favourably with a Welsh claret.
5. *1970 Côtes du Rod Laver*
Recommended by the Australian Wino Society, this has a kick on it like a mule. Eight bottles of this and you're really finished. At the opening of the Sydney Harbour Bridge Club they were fishing them out of the main sewers every half an hour.
6. *Perth Pink*
The most famous of the sparkling wines. This is a bottle with a message in it and the message is 'Beware.' This is not a wine for drinking. It's a wine for laying down and avoiding.
7. *Melbourne Old and Yellow*
Another good fighting wine, which is particularly heavy and should be used only for hand-to-hand combat.
8. *Château Chunder*
An appellation contrôlée specially grown for those keen on regurgitation. A fine wine which really opens up the sluices at both ends.
9. *Hôbart Runny*
For real emetic fans only. Should not be served during dinner.

ASHES **TO ASHES**

'The Final Test' (*La Testa*)
Director Pier Paolo Pasolini
Reviewed by Clive James.

Just as Peckinpah revealed the bloodthirsty violence bubbling beneath the skin of Edwardian man, so in a different way Pasolini rips off the MCC tie to reveal the seething cauldron of sex that lies beneath the white flannels and sweaty jockstraps of today's cricketers. This is a human interest picture: the sort that makes you concentrate on the usherette. All motion picture addicts should pin back their eyeballs and take a celluloid shower in this one. It may not be exactly your cup of possum juice, but catch it if you can for the sheer magic of the Intermission which comes like a dose of clap in the middle of a mad month in a Melbourne cathouse. *The Final Test* is a movie you'd be well-advised to miss. And you'd be wrong. Go and see it. You'll be surprised. It's terrible. It's definitely Hutton dressed as Alan Lamb, but I haven't had such an

Enforcing the follow-on at Trent Bridge

106

Amazing figures at Old Trafford

A rare picture of Pasolini at work during the filming of 'The Final Test'

England v Australia at Headingley

enjoyable time in the cinema since I spent four hours in a Sydney Drive-In and finally discovered it was a multi-storey car-park. Don't miss it. Avoid it like the plague. But go anyway. You'll hate it. It's marvellous. It's Kafka in a sheep dip, an example of the Protestant work ethic on rollerskates, with enough acres of fresh flesh to bring a boyish smile to the frozen features of a case-hardened Bushman at an outback cattle auction. But enough – as Kierkegaard observed – is a treat. Don't take your family, take your mac. It's smashing. You'll hate it. No sweat, but all armpit. Like sodomy, it's fun once in a while but let's hope they don't make it compulsory. Ouch.

HOW TO
WALK SILLY

ST BRIAN'S

I'd like to welcome all of you parents and boys, gathered here today. As you all know, St Brian's has a tradition of homosexuality stretching back over the past five hundred years. Boys from St Brian's have always been the most sought after in Business, Industry and the Church. We have produced homosexuals of many kinds and many talents, including no less than eight gay Chancellors of the Exchequer, two very pretty heads of the Coal Board and some really outrageous old Queens who have gone into the armed forces. Many schools frown on homosexuality amongst the boys, but we at St Brian's encourage it. Boys in the sixth form can stay on and take Advanced Feeling Up, Kissing 'A' Level and Really Getting To Know Each Other right up to University standard. During the summer all the lower forms are nude. And I personally think there is no finer sight than eleven sun-drenched pairs of buttocks walking onto a cricket square on a June afternoon. The curve of a young lad's . . . I'm sorry . . . I *do* apologise, I have the wrong notes.

I'd like to welcome all of you parents and boys gathered here today. As you all know, St Brian's has a tradition of academic excellence stretching back over five hundred years. Boys from St Brian's have always been the most sought after in Business, Industry and the Church. We have produced leaders of many kinds and of many talents including eight Chancellors of the Exchequer, no less than two heads of the Coal Board and many distinguished old boys who have gone into the armed forces. St Brian himself, as the magnificent East Window of this randy old . . . of this chapel reminds us was a penis . . . a pious and god-fearing man, whose words and thoughts have been passed down to us by scholars through the centuries . . . the school fees will be going up by £50 a term as from tomorrow . . . And it is through faith in Brian and Brian's example to us that this school has prospered and whacked little boys . . . and waxed over the years. I believe there is no finer school In the lower price range. Thank you.

THE UPPER-CLASS
TWIT OF THE YEAR
SHOW

The Greatest Upper-Class Race in the World

1. The Start
A difficult one is this. Many of the Twits fail to get off to any kind of start whatsoever. In 1967 a Captain Brough-Oyster was a faller on his way into the stadium, and tragically had to be put down.

2. The Straight Lines
The great thing is not to take these too fast. They can be coped with more easily if the Twit imagines they are Harrods corridors.

3. The Matchbox Jump
A good Twit will take this accidentally.

4. Kicking the Beggar
The field is beginning to stagger a lot here so you can take your time. The Judge can disqualify you if you kick the Beggar after he's down more than eight times. Many great Twits have gone out at this one simply through kicking the Judge. In 1947 O. K. S. J. St. P. Semaphore went out of racing altogether when he accidentally kicked three Irish Clergy and they set about him.

5. Hunt Ball Photograph
The Twit must face the Camera. He must also try and remember to kiss the Deb and not one of the other Twits.

Now come three easier obstacles; first:

6. Reversing into the Old Lady
An easy one this for the average Twit. Also, he is for once off his own worst enemy – his feet – and into an expensive automobile. Incidentally, a firm in Surbiton supplies the old ladies.

7. Slamming the Car Door to wake the Neighbour
Second nature to Kensington dwellers. County entrants might have a little difficulty here.

8. Insulting the Waiter
Again second nature, especially if the waiter's from a proper working-class home and not just a foreigner.

9. The Bar
Perhaps the most difficult after the Debs. They must walk under the bar without braining themselves. Most take 5 or 6 goes. The winning post is in sight now as they come to the tenth.

10. Shooting the Rabbits
They are of course tied down, but this in fact makes it more difficult as it removes the chance of the animals accidentally wounding themselves.

11. Taking the Bra off the Debs

Dummies are used nowadays as occasionally the Debs got excited. It's a good idea to let your Twits see a bra before the race.

12. Shooting themselves

This requires less skill than might be imagined, for Brigadier Henry Butcher in his History of the Race claims that nearly fifty per cent of all Twits are shot accidentally by the others. Still, they all count on the scorecard, and whilst the actual winner is probably stiffening somewhere back on the Course, there's many a second and third been picked up here at the final table.

Head: look for thickness. This is what makes for outstanding Twitting. Military training is an obvious advantage here.

The Face: look for absence of expression. Is he really vacant? If he is, make for the Tote.

Tie: an important clue to breeding. MCC ties are the favourite, closely followed by Eton, Harrow and the Guards.

Watch: probably ludicrously expensive. Probably stopped.

The naughty bits: are they completely dormant? Most of them are after leaving Public School but occasionally disasters occur. Simon Main Waring Waring Main had to be pulled off one of the dummies in 1969.

Feet: the best Twits try to keep as few on the ground as possible. Rugby helps.

Balance: a good Twit should have none whatsoever.

115

KASHMIR

The expedition: it's nightfall.

WOODERSON: Look, I don't know how to say this, Bunty . . .

BUNTY: What is it Doug?

WOODERSON: Well . . . well I'm feeling so bloody randy . . .

BUNTY: Randy?

WOODERSON: Yes, damn, damn randy . . . I don't know what to do . . .

BUNTY: Whereabouts?

WOODERSON: Mm? Well . . . just all over . . . All-consuming randiness . . .

BUNTY: Well the rains'll be here soon . . .

WOODERSON: The rains . . . ?

BUNTY: Yes that should help . . .

WOODERSON: I can't seem to get my mind off it. You know . . . Bunty, just this evening, I've been trying to do some calculations for tomorrow's march and every time I open the dividers I get this damn stirring . . .

BUNTY: The dividers?

WOODERSON: Yes . . . they're a lovely wooden pair pater gave me . . . As soon as I spread them apart, Bunty . . . As soon as I open the two –

BUNTY: Yes . . . yes . . . well I think when the rains come you'll feel better . . .

WOODERSON: Bunty . . . I don't think I can wait . . . I need a . . . oh god . . . I need a woman . . .

BUNTY: Well, this is the damn problem of being in one of the most lonely, inaccessible mountain ranges on earth, Doug.

WOODERSON: What about the bearers' wives?

BUNTY: I shouldn't if I were you, Douggie . . . It's not terribly done.

WOODERSON: There *must* be women in the Kashmir . . . somewhere . . .

BUNTY: Yes . . . but not in this bit, Doug . . . this is a terribly underpopulated . . . inhospitable area . . . I mean you may find a hill-tribe that –

WOODERSON: Where? Where?

BUNTY: But if you did, Douggie . . . you must remember they're all native . . . they do things differently out here.

WOODERSON: Not what *I* want to do, Bunty . . .

BUNTY: No, there's all sorts of marriage customs and betrothal and vows. You know, women are so different out here Douglas . . .

WOODERSON: Well *men* then . . . what about men?

BUNTY: Oh Douglas! Pull yourself together . . . and wait for the rains . . .

WOODERSON: You know that tiger outside . . .

BUNTY: You're not to *touch* that tiger . . . Douglas. It's not a tiger anyway . . .

WOODERSON: It's beautiful . . .

BUNTY: It's not beautiful . . .

WOODERSON: Well the chickens then . . .

BUNTY: They're for eating, Doug . . . you know that . . .

WOODERSON: *Before* we eat them . . . ! It doesn't affect the taste . . . honestly . . .

BUNTY: Shut up. Shut up. Wait for the rains . . . like we all do. For God's sake Douglas . . . you're not the only man in Kashmir who feels randy. But this is a scientific expedition . . . don't you realise that the vegetation changes revealed by the glacial recession only occur once or twice in a lifetime . . .

WOODERSON: I know; the goat! (*he gets up*)

BUNTY: (*stands, suddenly serious, he reaches for his service revolver*) Douglas . . . leave the goat alone . . .

WOODERSON: It's so friendly . . .

BUNTY: I know it's friendly, but it's the regimental mascot, Douglas, and if you lay one finger on that goat, I will blast you off the face of this earth . . .

WOODERSON: (*provocatively*) This sounds a little more than the regimental loyalty, Bunty . . . it's only a goat . . .

117

BUNTY: (*blushing furiously*) Denzil is not only a goat! Denzil stands for everything that I respect.

WOODERSON: It's not your goat . . .

BUNTY: It is the regiment's goat. Denzil and I have been together for as long as I've been in the 18th Foot. I remember him when he was a tiny little goat, scarcely able to walk, and I've looked after him on every expedition since then. Scarcely a day has gone by when I haven't thought about that goat. I love him, and I love the regiment.

WOODERSON: Love; that's what I need!

(*He starts to unbutton his jacket and make for the door*)

BUNTY: Not *that* sort of love . . . Wooderson . . . you pig. I mean the higher love that can exist between two people . . . or . . . or one person and a goat . . . who respect each other . . .

WOODERSON: (*picks up a box*) May I borrow your talc?

BUNTY: Wait for the rains!

WOODERSON: I can't.

(*He pulls off his jacket, sprinkles talc under his arms, and pushes his way out of the tent.* BUNTY *goes to the tent door and fires. Then he drops his head and shakes it sadly . . . He looks up . . . worried. Then speaks sharply to the* BEARER)

BUNTY: Kanke pura . . . Wooderson dak khane lao . . .
[Fetch me Wooderson's Dividers]
Fade.

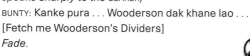

118

CHAOS THEORY
MADE E-Z

Somewhere in the Amazon, a butterfly flaps its wings.....

... causing a storm in New York that manages to delay an airplane landing at JFK....

.... causing a banker on board to miss an International Monetary Fund meeting.....

... CAUSING A DEBATE ON THE REFINANCING OF THE BRAZILIAN NATIONAL DEBT TO FAIL....

... CAUSING THE BRAZILIAN GOVERNMENT TO COLLAPSE....

... CAUSING AN ELECTION... RESULTING IN A NEW PRESIDENT WHO BOUGHT VICTORY WITH THE PROMISE OF FREE LAND IN THE AMAZONIAN RAINFOREST FOR THE SLUM DWELLERS OF RIO...

... CAUSING ONE LUCKY BENEFICIARY NAMED JORGE TO CLAIM, AND THEN CLEAR HIS LAND IN THE MOST EFFICIENT WAY AVAILABLE....

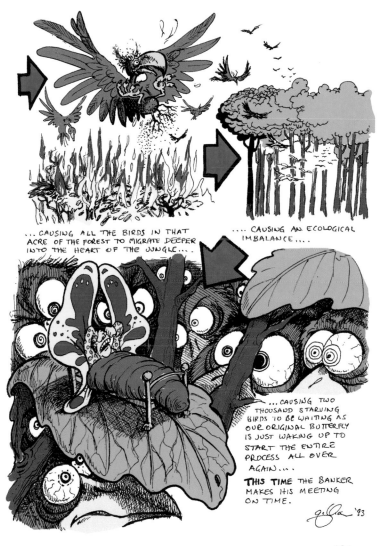

... CAUSING ALL THE BIRDS IN THAT ACRE OF THE FOREST TO MIGRATE DEEPER INTO THE HEART OF THE JUNGLE....

.... CAUSING AN ECOLOGICAL IMBALANCE....

... CAUSING TWO THOUSAND STARVING BIRDS TO BE WAITING AS OUR ORIGINAL BUTTERFLY IS JUST WAKING UP TO START THE ENTIRE PROCESS ALL OVER AGAIN...

THIS TIME THE BANKER MAKES HIS MEETING ON TIME.

'93

121

If you would like to buy the film rights for this page they are still available, at least up to the point of publication they were available. Obviously if we've sold the film rights to this page since publication then they are no longer available, unless of course you make a better offer than the one we have already accepted and in that way YOU can buy the film rights to this page. We always have hidden clauses or tricky legal loopholes in our contracts in the Film Business so we can get out of things if we change our minds. So having made your offer, and we having perfectly legally dodged out of any other agreement, you can now sit back content with your new 'property' as we film people call these things.

What are you getting for your money? Well quite simply you are getting the exclusive film rights for this page IN ITS ENTIRETY, including the page number, to film in whatever manner you wish. To hire and fire directors to film this page, to go to lunch with as many screenwriters as you want and tell them exactly how to write the screenplay for this page. You can, if you want, engage film stars to appear in the screen version of this page, including Bruce Willis, Cameron Diaz, Ewan MacGregor, Billy-Bob Thornton, Steve Buscemi, Gwyneth Paltrow, or even Salma Hayek. You may then lease the distribution rights of the finished film to Warner's, or Universal or even Harrods.

So just write to Python Productions enclosing a serious cheque and we will write back and tell you if your bid has been successful or whether we have already done a deal with Harvey Weinstein. Remember, ANYONE can be a film producer, all you need is money and a certain ruthlessness. See you at the Oscars . . .

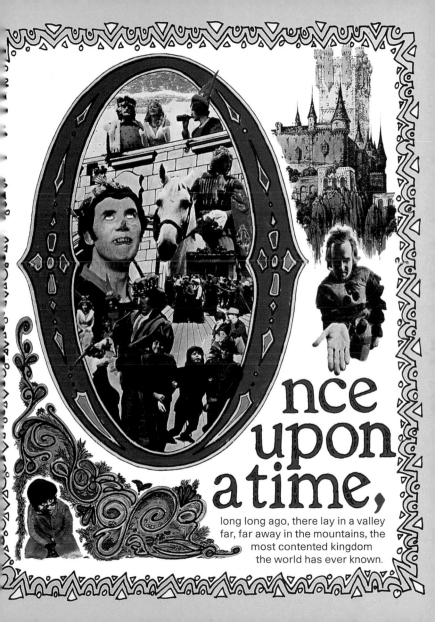

nce upon a time,

long long ago, there lay in a valley
far, far away in the mountains, the
most contented kingdom
the world has ever known.

It was called Happy Valley, and it was ruled over by a wise old King called Otto, and all his subjects flourished and were happy, and there were no discontents or grumblers, because Wise King Otto had had them all put to death along with the Trade Union leaders many years before. And all the good happy folk of Happy Valley sang and danced all day long, and anyone who was for any reason miserable or unhappy or who had any difficult personal problems was prosecuted under the Happiness Act.

And, while the good people of Happy Valley tenaciously frolicked away, their wise old King, who was a merry old thing, played strange songs on his Hammond Organ up in the beautiful castle, where he lived with his gracious Queen Syllabub and their lovely daughter Mitzi Gaynor, who had fabulous tits and an enchanting smile, and wooden teeth which she bought in a chemist's in Augsberg, despite the fire-risk. She treasured these teeth which were made of the finest pine and she varnished them after every meal. And next to her teeth her dearest love was her pet dog Hermann. She would take Hermann for long walks and pet and fuss over him all day long and steal him tasty titbits which he never ate, because sadly he was dead and no one had the heart to tell her because she was so sweet and innocent that she knew nothing of death or gastro-enteritis or even plastic hip joints. One day, while Mitzi was taking Hermann for a pull round the Royal Gardens, she set eyes on the most beautiful young man she had ever seen and fell head over heels in love with him, naturally assuming him to be a prince.

Well, as luck would have it, he *was* a prince, and so, after looking him up in the *Observer's Book of Princes* to discover his name, she went and introduced herself and the subject of marriage, and, in what seemed like the twinkling of an eye, but was in fact a fortnight, they were on their way to see King Otto, to ask his permission to wed. What a perfect couple they looked! Mitzi, resplendent in a delicate shell-pink satin brocade and some new bullet-proof mahogany teeth, and Prince Kevin, handsome as could be, drawing many an admiring glance from some randy old closet queens in the vestibule.

Soon they were at the door of the Kingdom-Ruling Room. And then, trying to control their excitement, they were ushered into the presence of the King himself, who sat at the Royal State Organ singing his latest composition, the strangely discordant 'Ya bim dee bim, thwackety f'tang stirkel boo bum.' And when the King had finished, some hours later, and the courtiers' applause had died down, Mitzi presented Prince Kevin, who bowed gracefully and asked the wise old King for his daughter's hand in marriage.

s he in the book?' asked the King.

'Oh yes, Daddy,' cried Mitzi.

'And do you love my daughter?' he queried, penetratingly.

'I do, sir!' replied Prince Kevin, and a ripple of delight passed round the room for already Kevin's princely bearing and sweetness of nature had won the entire court's approval.

'Good! But first, before I grant permission, I must set you a task that you may prove yourself worthy of my daughter's hand.'

'I accept!!' cried Kevin gallantly.

The old King's face grew grave. 'At nine o'clock tomorrow morning,' he explained, 'you must go to the top of the highest tower in this castle, and armed only with your sword, jump out of the window.'

And so, early the next day, the brave young prince, dressed in a

125

beautiful gold and white robe, and armed only with his magic sword, plummeted three hundred feet to a speedy death. How they all cheered! How funny the royal remains looked!

'Can we get married now, Daddy?' cried Mitzi, for, as we know, she knew nothing of death.

'No daughter, I'm afraid not,' answered the wise old King, although he was himself a necrophilia buff, 'he simply wasn't worthy of you.'

'Oh dear,' said Mitzi. 'Will he have to go in the ground like all the others?'

nd so most of Prince Kevin was buried alongside the remains of Prince Oswald (page 4 in the book) who'd had to fight an infantry division armed only with a copy of the *Guardian*; and Prince Robin (p. 19) who'd gallantly attempted to extinguish a fiery furnace by being thrown in it; and Prince Norbert (p. 36) who'd had to wrestle a combine harvester; and Prince Malcolm (p. 8) who'd had to catch a Boeing 747, but had dropped it.

So, the moment that Kevin's coffin had been laid to rest on the traditional huge black-edged Whoopee Cushion (for as Kevin was a prince, he had been granted a State Fancy Dress Funeral), Mitzi was off once again to the Royal Gardens, dragging the faithful Hermann behind her, to see if she could pull another prince. For princes had become extremely scarce; as rare, indeed, as an Australian virgin.

So Mitzi set off along the river bank, hopefully kissing frogs, until she spotted the slightest glint of gold from beneath a Giggling Willow Tree and running forward, espied – sure enough! – a prince. He was rather thin and spotty, with a long nose, and bandy legs, and nasty unpolished plywood

126

teeth, and a rare foot disease, but, thought Mitzi, a prince is a prince, and she fell in love with him without another thought.

And after a time, or a few times anyway, he, too, fell in love with her, and a few hours later they were on their way to ask King Otto's permission to wed, as this latest prince didn't read the newspapers any more than any of the others did, decadent, dimwitted, parasitic little bastards that they were.

'Is he in the book?' asked the King, surlily.

'Yes, Daddy,' cried Princess Mitzi, delightedly.

'Do you love my daughter?' queried the wise old King.

'Could be,' allowed Prince Walter, nasally.

'Do you,' continued the wise old King, 'want her hand in marriage?'

An uneasy silence fell upon the assembled courtiers, for none of them much cared for Walter's looks, not even the Lord Chancellor, who was extremely gay.

'. . . Yeah, all right.'

'In that case,' said the King, 'I must set you a task to prove you worthy of my daughter's hand.'

'Why?' came the bold reply.

'Because she's a fuckin' Princess, that's why,' explained the King, scarcely controlling his rage. 'And your task is that you must, quite unaided and unarmed, go down the town and get me twenty Marlboro.'

'What, now!?' exploded Walter.

'Not necessarily,' cried the King weakly, smiling round the court with all the easy spontaneity of a chat show host, 'I'll think about it.'

(*To be continued.*)

127

MR CHEEKY

NISUS WETTUS: Next? Crucifixion?

FIRST PRISONER: Yes.

NISUS WETTUS: Good . . . right. Out of the door, line on the left, one cross each . . . next . . . Crucifixion?

SECOND PRISONER: Yes.

NISUS WETTUS: Good . . . Out of the door, line on the left, one cross each . . . Next? Crucifixion?

MR CHEEKY: Er . . . no . . . freedom . . .

NISUS WETTUS: What?

MR CHEEKY: Er . . . freedom for me . . . They said I hadn't done anything so I could go free and live on an island somewhere.

NISUS WETTUS: Well, that's jolly good . . . In that case . . .

(*he goes to strike out Mr Cheeky's name*)

MR CHEEKY: No . . . no . . . it's crucifixion really. Just pulling your leg.

NISUS WETTUS: Oh . . . I see. Very good . . . out of the door, line on the . . .

MR CHEEKY: Yes . . . I know the way . . . out the door, line on the left, one cross each.

ALWAYS LOOK ON
THE BRIGHT SIDE OF
LIFE

MR CHEEKY: Cheer up, Brian. You know what they say . . .
Some things in life are bad
They can really make you mad
Other things just make you swear and curse.
When you're chewing on life's gristle
Don't grumble, give a whistle
And this'll help things turn out for the best . . .
And . . .
Always look on the bright side of life . . . (*whistle*)
Always look on the light side of life . . . (*whistle*)
If life seems jolly rotten
There's something you've forgotten
And that's to laugh and smile and dance and sing,
When you're feeling in the dumps,
Don't be silly chumps,
Just purse your lips and whistle – that's the thing.
And . . . always look on the bright side of life . . . (*whistle*)
Come on. (*others start to join in*)
Always look on the right side of life . . . (*whistle*)
For life is quite absurd
And death's the final word
You must always face the curtain with a bow.
Forget about your sin – give the audience a grin
Enjoy it – it's your last chance anyhow.

So . . . always look on the bright side of death
Just before you draw your terminal breath.
Life's a piece of shit
When you look at it,
Life's a laugh and death's a joke, it's true,
You'll see it's all a show,
Keep 'em laughing as you go
Just remember that the last laugh is on you.
And . . . always look on the bright side of life . . . (*whistle*)
Always look on the right side of life . . . (*etc).*

FOREWORD BY THE LATE
GRAHAM CHAPMAN

Sorry this foreword is a bit late. You can get a bit behind in the after life. There's so much time here it takes an eternity to do anything.

Many people go completely quiet after they are dead. But not me. In fact in the last few years I have released more books and records than the rest of the Pythons put together, and they aren't even dead yet. Mind you, that Cleese looked a bit frail last time I saw him on TV. Has he had some kind of facial work? And dear old Mickey Palin was looking a bit florid. All that travelling can't be good for him, and he was always a bit fond of the old Bordeaux. Gilliam has qualified for his bus pass and Jonesy looks quite decrepit. I'm told he can't even remember which one he was.

In fact only Eric Idle looks at all decent. I always fancied him. He was certainly the nicest of the lot. I miss him the most. I'm glad to see he has put together a selection of some of the gags and skits which once so amused the Nation. Fortunately tastes have matured over the years and so this sort of collection seems incredibly dated and certainly déja-vu all over again. But *Futuaris Nisi Irrisus Ridebis*, as we say up here. Fuck 'em if they can't take a joke.

Well, got to dash. A Mr Heisenberg is going to explain his Uncertainty Theory to God, which should be quite interesting as we are still unsure whether He exists or not. And they call this closure!

Love to you all,
Graham 'Doc' Chapman

SELECTED
BY
MICHAEL
PALIN

WITH A PREFACE BY JOHN CLEESE

I can remember very clearly the day Michael Palin joined the Python team. Several of the original members had started to move on: Aneurin Bevan at the end of the second series, and Laurens Van Der Post shortly after that; now Graham Greene had told us that he wanted to do only six more shows. So we were understandably very cheered by the sight of Michael's smiling, affable, slightly squat figure entering the rehearsal rooms to meet us, and it was a matter of only months before he was officially invited to join.

And what an impact he immediately made! We were all thrilled to have someone so eagerly bustling around, shining our shoes, running out for cigarettes and making us countless cups of coffee. And what most people don't realise is that, in addition to all this, he wrote some of the material that was used in the television series and, if memory serves me right, even appeared in a couple of sketches as a performer.

In fact the only drawback with Michael was the noise. If he has a fault, and he definitely does, it is that he veers towards the loquacious. Many of us enjoy conversation: Michael likes talking. He just can't get enough of it. He's a one-man 24 hour radio news station without the musical breaks. In fact, in the early seventies he twice reached the semi-finals of the All-England Talking Championships. And I'm confident that he would have won a championship, had he not suffered the misfortune to compete in the same era as the legendary Alyce Faye Eichelberger. So after a few weeks we persuaded him to wear at rehearsals a kind of oratorical muffling device, constructed by Graham Greene from a gas mask and a handgun silencer, which enabled the rest of us to get on with our work.

Imagine my surprise then, when one morning I entered a silent rehearsal room, assuming Michael had not yet arrived, and saw him sitting in the corner reading a book, as quiet as an artichoke. It was as startling a sight as Chapman arriving on time, or Gilliam having an insight, or Idle doing charity work, or Jones not holding a strong opinion about something, or Greene playing ice hockey. I tiptoed across the room to see what book had affected Michael so dramatically, and I read on its cover the one word – 'Abroad'. From the moment he put the book down the following day, he was hooked. The idea of abroad so fascinated him that from then on, he was almost always there, moving about it as much as possible, trying to find new bits.

So much so, that people speculated that this newly discovered wanderlust had displaced the old chatterlust. But it was not so; it was simply that Michael's constant wandering now presented him with the problem of whom to talk at. Fortunately this problem was neatly solved by his wife's suggestion that if a television crew were paid to accompany him he could rabbit interminably to them without the need, most of the time, to have any film in the camera.

As is well known, many of Michael's friends worried about this hyperactivity, despite the fact that it was giving his wife's eardrums time to regenerate; some felt it might mainly be a matter of diet, but I always believed it was psychological. So I decided to broach the subject with him, and, having chosen my moment carefully, I started by saying, 'Michael, a man can run and run for only so long but some day he has to turn round and face himself.' But already he was gone, off on another trip to cross Lake Titicaca on a pedalo. Thus were born *Around the World in 80 Days*, *Around the World in 79 Days*,

Around the World in 82 Days, and so on and so on and so on. People sometimes ask me 'Will Michael settle down some day?' Well, I sincerely believe he will. I can confidently see him, in another couple of decades, spending the day quietly driving round and round the M25, and then getting back home and putting his feet up in front of the fire to spend the rest of the evening with a good book and a TV crew. Let us hope that when this happens, his wife does not make the same error that she did last month when, coming across him in the bathroom, she called the police to report an intruder.

J.C.

Buenos Aires 1994

INTRODUCTION

Unlike the Spice Girls, the Monty Python team was formed by a triumph of unnatural selection. We were of many different heights, making group photographs tricky, and many different backgrounds – Graham Chapman had been a doctor, John Cleese a lawyer, Terry Gilliam a car mechanic, Eric Idle a Chelsea supporter and Terry Jones and myself the first to use the new toilets erected in Lambeth Walk, London in 1968.

The Spice Girls have another immeasurable advantage. They are naturally female. If the Pythons wanted to be female (which the work frequently demanded) we would have to engage in elaborate, often costly subterfuges, involving enormous padded brassières, reinforced high heels, shaved chests and make-up thick enough to disguise prodigious beard-growth. It's estimated that in portraying Mrs Thing on stage at the City Center, New York, Graham Chapman used over a ton of Revlon lipstick in an attempt to make Terry Jones laugh (and, less successfully, to try to become the New Face of Revlon).

In this little book I have trawled our work in an attempt to shed some light on the curious vagaries of history that threw people like us together and to see if there might be a lesson lurking here, a sign pointing towards some pattern for the future, a re-affirmation of the sublime ambition of the human spirit, a confirmation of the ineluctable destiny of mankind.

I came up with Knights who say "Ni", a Cheese Shop which has no cheese, a quiz for goats, a very long stage-direction and a song about a penis.

Sorry.

M.P. March 2000

ALL THINGS DULL & UGLY

All things dull and ugly,
All creatures short and squat,
All things rude and nasty,
The Lord God made the lot.

Each little snake that poisons,
Each little wasp that stings;
He made their brutish venom,
He made their horrid wings.
All things sick and cancerous,
All evil great and small,
All things foul and dangerous,
The Lord God made them all.

Each nasty little hornet,
Each beastly little squid;
Who made the spiky urchin,
Who made the sharks? He did.
All things scabbed and ulcerous,
All pox both great and small,
Putrid, foul and gangrenous,
The Lord God made them all.
Amen.

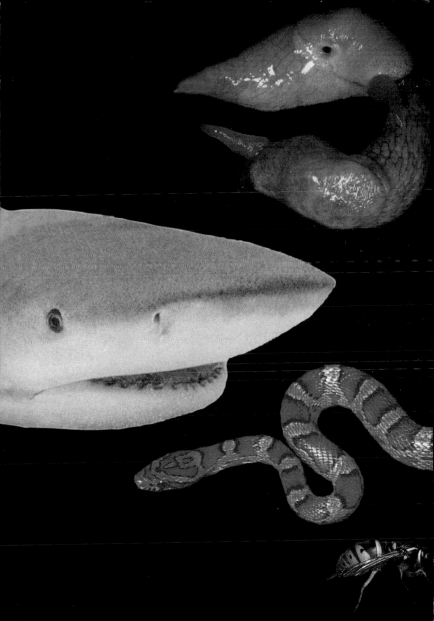

STIG O'TRACEY REMEMBERS
THE PIRANHA BROTHERS

INTERVIEWER: I've been told Dinsdale Piranha nailed your head to the floor.

STIG: No. Never. He was a smashing bloke. He used to buy his mother flowers and that. He was like a brother to me.

INTERVIEWER: But the police have film of Dinsdale actually nailing your head to the floor.

STIG: Oh yeah, he did that.

INTERVIEWER: Why?

STIG: Well he had to, didn't he? I mean there was nothing else he could do, be fair. I had transgressed the unwritten law.

INTERVIEWER: What had you done?

STIG: Er . . . well he didn't tell me that, but he gave me his word that it was the case, and that's good enough for me with old Dinsy. I mean, he didn't *want* to nail my head to the floor. I had to insist. He wanted to let me off. He'd do anything for you, Dinsdale would.

INTERVIEWER: And you don't bear him a grudge?

STIG: A grudge! Old Dinsy. He was a real darling.

INTERVIEWER: I understand he also nailed your wife's head to a coffee table. Isn't that true Mrs O'Tracy?

MRS O'TRACY: No, no, no, no, no, no, no, no, no, no.

STIG: Well he did do that, yeah. He was a hard man. Vicious but fair.

Vince Snetterton-Lewis agrees with this judgement.

VINCE: Yes, definitely he was fair. After he nailed me head to the table, I used to go round every Sunday lunchtime to his flat and apologise, and then we'd shake hands and he'd nail me head to the floor. He was very reasonable. Once, one Sunday I told him my parents were coming round to tea and would he mind very much not nailing my head that week and he agreed and just screwed my pelvis to a cake stand.

KING ARTHUR
GOES TO SEE THE GALAHADS

ARTHUR KING *is in a rather smart mock-tudor suburban avenue. He has a paper and is looking at it and checking house numbers. He finds a house and goes up a long driveway to a large mock-Tudor house. Lots of spyholes, burglar alarms, barred windows etc.*

He presses the bell. A pause. Someone comes to the door. A bolt slides back. Then another and another and another, a key turns in a lock another bolt, then a key, two more bolts, then the door opens a crack on a chain. A rather opulent-looking upper-class twit peers out. He is restraining an enormous Alsatian. . . .

ARTHUR: Mr Galahad?

GAI AHAD: Pronounced Ga'had, actually. Are you collecting for something, because I'd like to see some sort of official card, if you are . . .

WIFE *(off)*: Is it Jumble, darling? There's bags of stuff in the cellar.

ARTHUR: I'm looking for the Holy Grail.

GALAHAD: Ah wonderful, you saw the advert, then. Come in, come in. If you can just find your way through this bloody money . . .

GALAHAD *ushers* ARTHUR *into an opulent hall with a six-inch layer of banknotes everywhere.*

. . . that's the damn trouble of working in property . . . you amass such vast sums of loot that it's difficult to know where to put it. The cottage in Chelsea's being done up as a safe for when we're in town and we've bought a super little plot in Wales where we're going to sink a strongbox . . . then we can get rid of all this bloody stuff.

The scene ends with ARTHUR *being given a Holy Grail by the* GA'HADS. *They put it in a carrier bag for him and he takes it away.*

GOATS CORNER

Hello, goats! First a quiz:

Quiz

1. How many goats have stood for Parliament?

a) 1

b) 70

c) none

2. What animal can swallow a sheep whole?

a) a goat

b) an anaconda

3. Who was the famous Notts and England fast bowler who figured in the body-line controversy of the early 1930s?

a) Harold Larwood

b) a goat

4. Which goat wrote "Oliver Twist"?

a) Smokey

b) Billy Boy

c) Jacko

d) Tin-Tin

e) Not a goat at all

Answers

1. 70

2. an anaconda

3. Harold Larwood

4. Jacko thought up the title but *obviously* didn't write the book

Quotes about goats

What Famous People have said about Goats:

a) Milton: nothing

b) Robespierre: nothing

c) Dante: nothing

d) William Pitt the Elder: "I must go and put a goat on" (poss. misheard – Ed.)

e) Henry Ford: nothing

f) Clodagh Rodgers: nothing

g) Keith Miller (Great Australian all-rounder of the 1950s): nothing

Where to eat in London for Goats

a) Hyde Park

b) Regent's Park

c) Hampstead Heath

d) The Quality Restaurant, Tottenham Street

A message from Tonto

Once again it's been a bad year for goats, with humans confirming their ascendency in the vital fields of politics, economics, education and technological achievements. Only in the Arts and in the mountains have goats maintained their supremacy. Eton, Harrow and many other top public schools are still closed to goats, and, of the Services, only the R.A.F. allows goats to take up anything other than short-service commissions. Fashion still passes us by, and when did you last see a goat on Top Of The Pops?

If we are to change this at all, we must learn to THINK GOAT. Don't think of yourself as the plaything of Alpine milkmaids, the mascot of the Irish Guards . . . Think of yourself as a GOAT. Don't be compromised by the R.S.P.C.A. . . . remember GOAT IS GREAT!

Right on!

    yours *Tonto*

P.S. Do not eat this message

148

THE **HEALED LOONEY**

MOTHER: Well, how does it feel to be cured then?

SON: All right.

MOTHER: Your father and I spent a great deal of money getting you to Jerusalem.

SON: Yes. Thank you.

MOTHER: It wasn't easy for us you know. A lot of our friends didn't agree with what we did. I mean, we're not the sort of people to jostle around in crowds.

SON: No.

MOTHER: You were a looney you know. You were stark raving mad. You thought you were a bat.

SON: Oh?

MOTHER: Oh yes . . . you used to run around flapping and making strange high-pitched noises. You used to crouch on top of

149

cupboards and hiss at people.

SON: Oh.

MOTHER: Yes, you were very bad, wasn't he Miriam?

AUNTIE MIRIAM: Oh yes. *(She carries on laying out the cakes rather pathetically.)*

MOTHER: Well, maybe you'll be able to help around the house a bit now. Help your mother.

AUNTIE MIRIAM *hands around the cakes.*

AUNTIE MIRIAM: Jesus seemed quite a nice man.

MOTHER: Oh yes, very pleasant. We had a little chat about schools. *Suddenly the* SON *makes a strange high-pitched squeak. They all turn.*

MOTHER: What's the matter with you?

SON: Nothing Mummy, I just felt a little like a bat.

MOTHER: You didn't!

AUNTIE MIRIAM: Oh dear.

SON: Only a little. I just felt a little bat-like just for a moment.

MOTHER: *How* bat-like?

SON: Just for a moment I thought I was airborne again, winging my sightless way from eave to eave . . . that's all.

MOTHER: Well you're not a bat any more. Are you Paul? You *know* that.

SON: Oh yes, Mummy, but I still wish I was sometimes.

FATHER *enters.*

FATHER: How are you Paul?

SON: Fine, thank you Daddy.

FATHER *glances at* MOTHER.

FATHER: Well, good. Delicious cakes I must say, Auntie Miriam.

AUNTIE MIRIAM: I bought them in Jerusalem.

150

FATHER: Oh, well they're very tasty.

MOTHER *(sharply)*: Where are you going?

SON: I'm going to eat my cake up on the cupboard.

He pulls a chair over and starts to mount the cupboard.

MOTHER *(to FATHER)*: What did I tell you!

FATHER: Well, yes, but he is much better dear.

MOTHER: What d'you mean – *"better"*!

FATHER: Well, I mean there's not necessarily anything wrong in wanting to eat his cakes on the cupboard.

MOTHER *(voice rising)*: Of course there is you silly man! No rational, sane person goes and eats their cakes on top of a cupboard!

FATHER: Er . . . Paul. Paul!

The son is just climbing on to the top of the cupboard.

FATHER: Paul, why are you going to eat your cake on top of the cupboard?

SON: It's more comfortable up here, Daddy. Do you mind?

FATHER: Well, your mother and I would prefer it if you came and ate at the table with us.

SON: Oh, all right.

He gets down and comes over to the table.

SON: Is that what I used to do when I was a bat?

FATHER *(quickly)*: Well yes, you used to do some strange things, dear, but now it's all over.

SON: Oh yes, I don't think I'm a bat any more.

FATHER: No.

SON *(after a pause during which the atmosphere has relaxed a bit)*: It's funny really, both my parents being bats and me not being a bat.

(Father screams and throws a scroll at him)

EGON RONAY'S GOOD PEOPLE GUIDE

41% **Mr & Mrs Grayson**
Swindon
Wiltshire Map 24
19 Edworth Road
Swindon 262
First reports of this middle-aged couple were not good,
but since inclusion in the Guide last year their standards
have improved. Though Mr Grayson remains rather dull,
his wife is well worth a visit if you're in the neighbourhood.

69% **Mr & Mrs Rogers, Brianette**
& Granny
Swindon
Wiltshire Map 24
21 Edworth Road
Swindon 701
A pleasant little family, Mr & Mrs Rogers are cheerful despite
financial difficulties and always good for a chat. Brianette is a well-
developed eighteen-year-old and Granny is deaf. Avoid the back
sitting-room.

80% **Doreen & Arthur Henbison**
Bletchley
Bedfordshire Map 36
6B The Flats
Bletchley 9041
At last what Bletchley has lacked for years, a really exciting couple. Arthur is an ex-hypnotist, and Doreen in the WAAF. They introduced wife-swapping to the flats four years ago and now it's hard to get in. Must book – especially at weekends.

18% **Mr & Mrs Potter**
Worthing
Sussex Map 18
88 Rockery Crescent
Worthing 204
An appalling couple, rude and short-tempered. Their kitchen is painted a frightful yellow and Mr Potter is an uncompromising Marxist.

THE CHEESE SHOP

MOUSEBENDER: Now my good man, some cheese, please.

WENSLEYDALE: Yes certainly, sir. What would you like?

M: Well, how about a little Red Leicester?

W: I'm afraid we're fresh out of Red Leicester, sir.

M: Oh never mind. How are you on Tilsit?

W: Never at the end of the week, sir. Always get it fresh first thing on Monday.

M: Tish, tish. No matter. Well, four ounces of Caerphilly, then, if you please, stout yeoman.

W: Ah, well, it's been on order for two weeks, sir, I was expecting it this morning.

M: Yes, it's not my day is it. Er, Bel Paese?

W: Sorry.

M: Red Windsor.

W: Normally sir, yes, but today the van broke down.

M: Ah. Stilton?

W: Sorry.

M: Gruyère, Emmental?

W: No.

M: Any Norwegian Jarlsberger?

W: No.

M: Liptauer?

W: No.

M: Lancashire.

W: No.

M: White Stilton?

W: No.

M: Danish Blue?

W: No.

M: Double Gloucester?

W: . . . No.

M: Cheshire?

W: No.

M: Any Dorset Blue Vinney?

W: No.

M: Brie, Rocquefort, Pont-l'Évêque, Port Salut,

Savoyard, Saint-Paulin, Carre-de-L'Est, Boursin, Bresse-Bleue, Perle de Champagne, Camembert?

W: Ah! We do have some Camembert, sir.

M: You do. Excellent.

W: It's a bit runny, sir.

M: Oh, I like it runny.

W: Well as a matter of fact it's *very* runny, sir.

M: No matter. No matter. Hand over le fromage de la Belle France qui s'appelle Camembert, s'il vous plaît.

W: I think it's runnier than you like it, sir.

M *(smiling grimly)*: I don't care how excrementally runny it is. Hand it over with all speed.

W: Yes, sir. *(bends below the counter and reappears)* Oh . . .

M: What?

W: The cat's eaten it.

M: Has he?

W: She, sir.

M: Gouda?

W: No.

M: Edam?

W: No.

M: Caithness?

W: No.

M: Smoked Austrian?

W: No.

M: Sage Derby?

W: No, sir.

M: You do have some
cheese, do you?

W: Certainly, sir. It's a cheese shop, sir. We've got . . .

M: No, no, no, don't tell me. I'm keen to guess.

W: Fair enough.

M: Wensleydale?

W: Yes, sir?

M: Splendid. Well, I'll have some of that then, please.

W: Oh, I'm sorry sir, I thought you were referring to me, Mr
Wensleydale.

M: Gorgonzola?

W: No.

M: Parmesan?

W: No.

M: Mozzarella?

W: No.

M: Pippo Crème?

W: No.

M: Any Danish Fynbo?

W: No.

M: Czechoslovakian Sheep's Milk Cheese?

W: No.

M: Venezuelan Beaver Cheese?

W: Not today sir, no.

M: Well let's keep it simple, how about Cheddar?

W: Well I'm afraid we don't get much call for it around these parts.

M: No call for it? It's the single most popular cheese in the world!

W: Not round these parts, sir.

M: And pray what is the most popular cheese round these parts?

W: Ilchester, sir.

M: I see.

W: Yes, sir. It's quite staggeringly popular in the manor, squire.

M: Is it?

W: Yes sir, it's our number-one seller.

M: Is it?

W: Yes, sir.

M: Ilchester eh?

W: Right.

M: OK, I'm game. Have you got any, he asked expecting the answer no?

W: I'll have a look sir . . . nnnnnnooooooooo.

M: It's not much of a cheese shop really, is it?

W: Finest in the district, sir.

M: And what leads you to that conclusion?

W: Well, it's so clean.

M: Well, it's certainly uncontaminated by cheese.

Dear Madame Palm,
I have a teensy problemette. As I was mincing down the road-poady
the other Davy daykins, I saw an absolutely divine, but divine *darling-*
heart!, jackety-poohs in ever so soft Sammy silk. Ooh! It drove me
delirious ducky-darling, but when could I wear it?
The Rev. B. J. Mitchell,
Upper Choirboy, Gloucs.

Arson is a perfectly natural feeling, Geoffrey. How many of us at one
time or another in our lives hasn't felt the need to set fire to some
great public building or other. I know I have.

Dear Madame Palm,
I have a problem. You see I have bad breath. Also I am quite ugly. I
am so embarrassed about this and I don't know who else to turn to
for confidential advice. I am too shy to ask my family doctor and I
would just die if anyone ever found out.
NAME AND ADDRESS SUPPLIED.
(Although in fact it is:

Betty Rogers,
32, The Cuttings, Bolton.
Telephone Number: Bolton 0123495)

Dear Betty, how many times must I keep telling you that sex is fun. I
like it. You like it. Everybody likes it. Mr Robinson from the off-licence
likes it twice.

THE **PROBLEM** WITH **SPANISH HOLIDAYS**

A would-be tourist explains his preferences to DEREK BOUNDER, *a travel agent.*

TOURIST: I'm fed up going abroad and being treated like sheep, what's the point of being carted round in buses, surrounded by sweaty mindless oafs from Kettering and Boventry in their cloth caps and their cardigans and their transistor radios and their "Sunday Mirrors", complaining about the tea, "Oh they don't make it properly here, do they, not like at home," stopping at Majorcan bodegas selling fish and chips and Watney's Red Barrel and calamares and two veg and sitting in cotton sun frocks squirting Timothy White's suncream all over their puffy raw swollen purulent flesh cos they "overdid it on the first day"!

BOUNDER *(agreeing patiently)*: Yes. Absolutely, yes, I quite agree . . .

TOURIST: And being herded into endless Hotel Miramars and Bellevueses and Bontinentals with their international luxury modern roomettes and their Watney's Red Barrel and their swimming pools full of fat German businessmen pretending to be acrobats and forming pyramids and frightening the children and barging into the queues and if you're not at your table spot on seven you miss your bowl of Campbell's Cream of Mushroom soup, the first item on the menu of International Cuisine, and every Thursday night there's bloody cabaret in the bar featuring some tiny emaciated dago with nine-inch hips and some big fat bloated tart with her hair Brylcreemed down and a big arse presenting Flamenco for Foreigners.

BOUNDER *(beginning to get fed up)*: Yes, yes, now . . .

TOURIST: And then some adenoidal typists from Birmingham with diarrhoea and flabby white legs and hairy bandy-legged wop waiters called Manuel, and then once a week there's an excursion to the local Roman ruins where you can buy cherryade and melted ice cream and bleedin' Watney's Red Barrel, and then one night they take you to a local restaurant with local colour and colouring and they show you there and you sit next to a party of people from Rhyl who keeps singing "Torremolinos, Torremolinos", and complaining about the food, "Oh! It's so greasy isn't it?" and then you get cornered by some drunken greengrocer from Luton with an Instamatic and Dr Scholl sandals and Tuesday's *Daily Express* and he drones on and on and on about how Mr Smith should be running this country and how many languages Enoch Powell can speak and then he throws up all over the Cuba Libres.

BOUNDER: Will you be quiet please.

TOURIST: And sending tinted postcards of places they don't know they haven't even visited, "to all at number 22, weather wonderful, our room is marked with an 'X'. Wish you were here."

BOUNDER: Shut up.

TOURIST: "Food very greasy but we have managed to find this marvellous little place hidden away in the back streets."

BOUNDER: Shut up!

TOURIST: "Where you can even get Watney's Red Barrel and cheese and onion . . ."

BOUNDER: Shut up!!!

TOURIST: ". . . crisps and the accordionist plays 'Maybe it's because I'm a Londoner'" and spending four days on the tarmac at Luton airport on a five-day package tour with nothing to eat but dried Watney's sandwiches . . .

BOUNDER: Shut your bloody gob! I've had enough of this, I'm going to ring the police.

A corner of a police station. One policeman is knitting, another is making a palm tree out of old newspapers. The phone rings.

KNITTING POLICEMAN: Oh . . . take it off the hook.

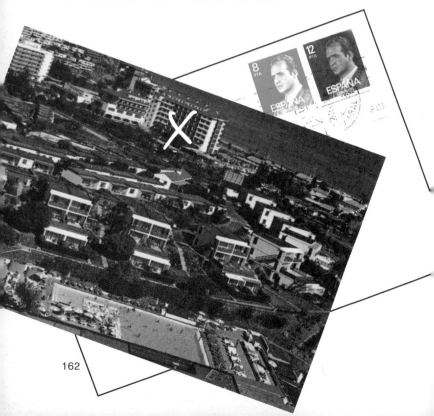

PORT SHOEM
BY THE SPEVEREND ROONER

I've a grouse and harden in the country,
An ace I call my plown,
A treat I can replace to
When I beed to knee alone.
Catterfly and butterpillar
Perch on beefy lough,
And I listen to the dats and cogs
As they mark and they biaow.
Yes wature here is nunderful,
There is no weed for nords,
While silling by my windowflutter
Biny little tirds.

The Stratton Indicator

Permission to build new garden shed refused

Mr Leonard Whim (39), a local man, today attacked the decision of the Town Borough Council to refuse him permission to construct another garden shed near his £10,000 house in lower Ching, on the grounds that he already had one shed. 'This is worse than living in a communist state' Mr Leonard told one of our reporters. 'To my mind it's creeping socialism. I fought in the war for freedom to build garden sheds when and where you wanted.

Mrs Whim, 32, a trim, petite, blonde wearing a matching tweed costume in striking aquamarine with elegant lace-up boots, and a fiery rose hat, agreed, said a neighbour. Leonard Whim is well-known in the area and has two dogs.

A Councillor defended the decision amidst angry scenes outside the 17th Century 'Clatch', which is shortly to be demolished to make way for a new car-park. 'This whole thing' he said 'has been blown up out of all proportion. Although one or two members of the Council were quite frankly a little unhappy about Mr Whim's plans to build a box-girder garden shed with split-level shopping piazza, covered walk-way, underground garage-cum-swimming pool, with facilities for all-night split-level shopping, and a split-level entertainment centre complete with bowling alley and split-level bingo hall.'

Press on

'I shall press on' said Mr Whim to journalists. 'I intend to convince the Council that they are wrong. This garden shed is going to be built, and when they see the Architect's presents I'm sure they will change their minds.' Mr Whim is head of a large road haulage firm and building works and has had many successful contracts with the Council.

WINNER OF THE LONGEST STAGE DIRECTION EVER

Long John Silver disappears. A pause. Two boxers appear. They circle each other. On one's head a bowler hat appears, vanishes. On the other's a stove-pipe hat appears. On the first's head a fez. The stove-pipe hat becomes a stetson. The fez becomes a cardinal's hat. The stetson becomes a wimple. Then the cardinal's hat and the wimple vanish. One of the boxers becomes Napoleon and the other boxer is astonished. Napoleon punches the boxer with the hand inside his jacket. The boxer falls, stunned. Horizontally he shoots off stage.

Shot of cat, watching unimpressed.

Napoleon does a one-legged pixilated dance across the stage and off, immediately reappearing on the other side of stage doing the same dance in the same direction. He reaches the other side, but is halted by a traffic policeman. The policeman beckons on to the stage a man in a penguin skin on a pogostick. The penguin gets half way across and then turns into a dustbin. Napoleon hops off stage. The policeman goes to the dustbin, opens it and Napoleon gets out.

Shot of cat, still unmoved.

A nude man with a towel round his waist gets out of the dustbin. Napoleon points at the ground. A chair appears where he points. The nude man gets on to the chair, jumps in the air and vanishes. Then Napoleon points to the ground by him and a small cannon appears. Napoleon fires the cannon and the policeman disappears. The man with the towel round his waist gets out of the dustbin and is chased off stage by the penguin on the pogostick. A sedan chair is carried on

166

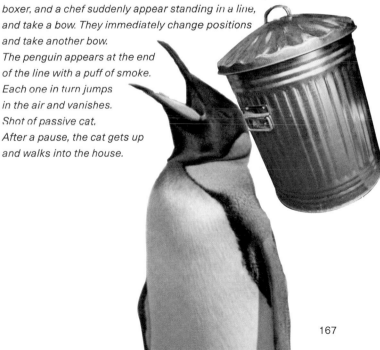

stage by two chefs. The man with the towel gets out
and the penguin appears from the dustbin and chases
him off. Napoleon points to the sedan chair and it
changes into a dustbin. The man in the towel runs back on to the
stage and jumps in the dustbin. He looks out and the penguin
appears from the other dustbin and hits him on the head with a raw
chicken.
Shot of cat still unimpressed.
Napoleon, the man with the towel round his waist, the policeman, a
boxer, and a chef suddenly appear standing in a line,
and take a bow. They immediately change positions
and take another bow.
The penguin appears at the end
of the line with a puff of smoke.
Each one in turn jumps
in the air and vanishes.
Shot of passive cat.
After a pause, the cat gets up
and walks into the house.

167

MIDDLEWORD
BY E.F. GOD

When I created the world in those *amazingly* busy seven days, I remember it as being a tremendously exciting period. There was *so* much to do that I honestly had hardly any time to notice what I was creating. I know that sounds awful, but I think anyone who's created anything will realise that very often you become so tied up with whatever it is you're creating that you can't see the wood for the trees – and I was *creating* the wood and the trees!

I mean, some days were great. The first day, of course, we couldn't see a bloody thing. I mean, I actually had to invent light just so we could see what we were doing! Sounds crazy now, doesn't it! Once I'd got the hang of it and done the basics there were some very exciting moments, though. The firmament, which I did on the second day, was great because, to be quite honest, I had no idea what a firmament really was, I just had to have something to divide the waters from the waters, and it turned out to be just right for that purpose. I also liked the tree yielding fruit. I don't know, it just had a nice ring to it. I suppose, now, with the benefit of hindsight, perhaps I should have just stuck to the tree and forgotten the fruit, but I liked the fruit and I didn't know Adam and Eve would make such a bollocks of it (excuse my French). I've been quite criticised over the years for letting them loose in the Garden of Eden, but I gave them Free Will and they decided that rather than write poetry or sing to each or invent a board game they'd go and talk to snakes. All right, I accept that there was an inherent risk but honestly, if you could have the choice to do anything you wanted in the loveliest garden ever made, with rivers and trees yielding fruit all over the place, would you seek out the nearest snake and ask how you could best get a rise out of the park-keeper? The next thing is that poor old Muggins is being blamed for everything from the Black Death to setting fire to Windsor Castle. There is no evidence in any of my utterances that I tampered with the wiring in the Long Gallery, just below the little French satinwood side-table where the Queen keeps the telephone directories, and if you can find the phrase "And then God created buboes", then all right, I decimated Europe, personally, in the fourteenth century. (I mean, I *created* Europe in the first place, why would I want to decimate it?) Sorry to go on but there is a downside to being Creator (my capitals).

ISN'T IT AWFULLY NICE
TO HAVE A PENIS

NOËL COWARD: Good evening ladies and gentlemen. Here's a little number I tossed off recently in the Caribbean.

Isn't it awfully nice to have a penis,
Isn't it frightfully good to have a dong?
It's swell to have a stiffy,
It's divine to own a dick,
From the tiniest little tadger,
To the world's biggest prick.

So three cheers for your Willy or John Thomas,
Hooray for your one-eyed trouser snake,
Your piece of pork, your wife's best friend,
Your Percy or your cock,
You can wrap it up in ribbons,
You can slip it in your sock,
But don't take it out in public,
Or they will stick you in the dock,
And you won't come back.

THE ALL-ENGLAND SUMMARIZE PROUST COMPETITION

Showbiz music, applause, and ARTHUR MEE *appears from the back of the stage; he wears the now traditional spangly jacket.*

MEE: Good evening and welcome, or as Proust would say, "la malade imaginaire de recondition et de toute surveillance est bientôt la même chose". *(Roars of applause)* Remember each contestant this evening has a maximum of fifteen seconds to sum up "A La Recherche du Temps Perdu" and on the Proustometer over here . . . *(A truly enormous, but cheap, audience appreciation gauge; it lists the seven books of Proust's masterwork in the form of a thermometer)* you can see exactly how far he gets. So let's crack straight on with our first contestant tonight. He's last year's semi-finalist from Luton – Mr Harry Bagot.

BAGOT *in evening dress, comes forward from back of stage, he has a number three on his back.*

Hello Harry. You're on the summarizing spot. You have fifteen seconds from *now.*

BAGOT: Proust's novel ostensibly tells of the irrevocability of time lost, the forfeiture of innocence through experience, the reinstatement of extra-temporal values of time regained; ultimately the novel is both optimistic and set within the context of a humane religious experience, re-stating as it does the concept of intemporality. In the first volume, Swann, the family friend visits . . .

Gong goes. Chord of music, applause.

The meter has hardly risen at all.

MEE: Well tried, Harry.

VOICE OVER: A good attempt there but unfortunately he chose a

general appraisal of the work, before getting on to the story and, as you can see, *(close up of Proustometer)* he only got as far as page one of "Swann's Way", the first of the seven volumes. A good try though and very nice posture.

MEE: Now Harry what made you first want to try and start summarizing Proust?

BAGOT: Well I first entered a seaside Summarizing Proust Competition when I was on holiday in Bournemouth, and my doctor encouraged me with it.

MEE: And Harry, what are your hobbies outside summarizing?

BAGOT: Well, strangling animals, golf and masturbating.

MEE: Well, thank you Harry Bagot.

BAGOT *walks off-stage. Music and applause.*

VOICE OVER: Well there he goes. Harry Bagot. He must have let himself down a bit on the hobbies, golf's not very popular around here, but never mind, a good try.

MEE: Thank you ladies and gentlemen. Mr Rutherford from Leicester, are you ready Ronald? *(RONALD is a very eager man in tails)* Right. On the summarizing spot. You have got fifteen seconds from now.

RONALD: Er, well, Swann, Swann, there's this house, there's this house, and er, it's in the morning, it's in the morning – no, it's the evening, in the evening and er, there's a garden and er, this bloke comes in – bloke comes in – what's his name – what's his name, er just said it – big bloke – Swann, Swann . . .

The gong sounds.

MEE: Well ladies and gentlemen, I don't think any of our contestants this evening have succeeded in encapsulating the intricacies of Proust's masterwork, so I'm going to award the first prize this evening to the girl with the biggest tits.

The Stratton Indicator

Stratton go top of the League

By defeating arch-rivals neighbouring Cubsy by one run on Saturday Stratton go top of the Grisdale League, two points ahead of Sudsy and Wells. The main feature of their victory was a superb innings by local man skipper Hemsley who held off the Cubsy bowlers when the match seemed to be swinging their way. Details of the Match

---

Cubsy

Groat c. & b. Wilkes	0
Sprange l.b.w., b. Wilkes	0
Thompson J. run out	1
Caryotid P. st. Si, b. Rant	0
Flake c. Limp, b. Wilkes	0
Tickersley not out	0
Watt J. l.b.w., b. Rant	0
Armstrong B. c. Rotter, b. Wilkes	0
Fletcher N. b. Rant	0
Thompson E. ht. wkt., b. Parkes	0
Extras	1
Total—All Out	

Stratton

Parkes b. Thompson	0
Si c. & b. Caryotid	0
Rant P. not out	0
Rotter b. Thompson	0
Limp rtd. hurt	
Wilkes c. Watt, b. Caryotid	0
Cooke C. l.b.w., b. Watt	0
Cook P. b. Caryotid	0
Sampson R. st. Flake, b. Groat	2
Hemsley not out	0
Extras	1
	2
Total for nine	

THE ARCHITECT
SKETCH

CHAIRMAN: Gentlemen, we have two basic suggestions for the design of this residential block, and I thought it best that the architects themselves came in to explain the advantages of both designs. *(A knock at the door)* That must be the first architect now. *(*MR WIGGIN *comes in)* Ah, yes   it's Mr Wiggin of Ironside and Malone.
WIGGIN *walks to the table on which his model stands.*
MR WIGGIN: Good morning, gentlemen. This is a twelve-storey block combining classical neo-Georgian features with all the advantages of modern design. The tenants arrive in the entrance hall here, are carried along the corridor on a conveyor belt in extreme comfort and past murals depicting Mediterranean scenes, towards the rotating knives. The last twenty feet of the corridor are heavily soundproofed. The blood pours down these chutes and the mangled flesh slurps into these . . .
FIRST CITY GENT: Excuse me . . .
MR WIGGIN: Hm?
FIRST CITY GENT: Did you say knives?
MR WIGGIN: Rotating knives, yes.
SECOND CITY GENT: Are you proposing to slaughter our tenants?
MR WIGGIN: Does that not fit in with your plans?
FIRST CITY GENT: No, it does not. We wanted a simple block of flats.
MR WIGGIN: Oh, I see. I hadn't correctly divined your attitude towards your tenants. You see I mainly design slaughterhouses. Yes, pity. Mind you this is a real beaut. I mean, none of your blood caked on the walls and flesh flying out of the windows, inconveniencing passers-by with this one. I mean, my life has been building up to this.
SECOND CITY GENT: Yes, and well done. But we did want a block of flats.

177

MR WIGGIN: Well, may I ask you to reconsider? I mean, you wouldn't regret it. Think of the tourist trade.

FIRST CITY GENT: No, no, it's just that we wanted a block of flats, not an abattoir.

MR WIGGIN: Yes, well, of course, that's just the sort of blinkered philistine pig ignorance I've come to expect from you non-creative garbage. You sit there on your loathsome, spotty behinds squeezing blackheads, not caring a tinker's cuss about the struggling artist. *(shouting)* You excrement! You lousy hypocritical whining toadies with your lousy colour TV sets and your Tony Jacklin golf clubs and your bleeding masonic handshakes! You wouldn't let me join, would you, you blackballing bastards! Well I wouldn't become a freemason now if you went down on your lousy, stinking, purulent knees and begged me.

SECOND CITY GENT: Well, we're sorry you feel like that but we, er, did want a block of flats. Nice though the abattoir is.

MR WIGGIN: Oh *(blows raspberry)* the abattoir, that's not important. But if one of you could put in a word for me I'd love to be a freemason. Freemasonry opens doors. I mean, I was . . . I was a bit on edge just now, but if I was a mason I'd just sit at the back and not get in anyone's way.

FIRST CITY GENT: Thank you.

MR WIGGIN: I've got a second-hand apron.

SECOND CITY GENT: Thank you.

MR WIGGIN *(going to the door but stopping)*: I nearly got in at Hendon.

FIRST CITY GENT: Thank you.

NEVER BE RUDE TO AN ARAB

a plea for tolerance and understanding
(in a world full of fucking loonies)

Never be rude to an Arab,
An Israeli, or Saudi, or Jew,
Never be rude to an Irishman
No matter what you do.
Never poke fun at a Nigger,
A Spik, or a Wop, or a Kraut,
And never put DOWN . . .

THE
MARTYRDOM
OF ST BRIAN

And it came to pass that St Brian was taken from his place to another place where he was lain upon pillows of silk and made to rest himself amongst sheets of muslin and velvet, and there stroked was he by maidens of the Orient. Full sixteen days and nights stroked they him, yea verily and caressed him. His hair ruffled they and their fingers rubbed they in oil of olives and ran them across all parts of his body forasmuch as to soothe him. And the soles of his feet licked they and the upper parts of his thigh did they anoint with the balm of forbidden trees, and with the teeth of their mouths nibbled they the pointed bits at the top of his ears, yea verily and did their tongues thereof make themselves acquainted with his secret places. For fifteen days and nights did Brian withstand these maidens, but on the sixteenth day he cried out, saying: "This is fantastic!" "Oh! this is terrific!" And the Lord did hear the cry of Brian and verily he came down and slew the maidens and their jars of oil tipped he over and he caused their cotton wool to blow away. Then he sent down seven dark stallions carrying seven mighty warriors who did breathe fire about the place where Brian had lain, so the soft furnishings thereof perished – and Brian carried he up amongst the clouds to remain with him forever. And Brian in his anguish cried out that the Lord was a rotten bastard, but the Lord heard his cry and forgave He him and Brian did rest with the angels.

But it came to pass that Brian's fingers could not be still, and male and female poked he them. And the angel of the Lord saw that Brian's fingers were full of naughtiness, and he spake unto Brian, saying: "Thy fingers are full of naughtiness and they have become like unto great big adders in the sight of the Lord." And Brian knew that his fingers had sinned, and he went unto an high place and was ashamed. And the angel of the Lord came to Brian and laid his arm upon him and spake unto him: "Fear not Brian, for if thou eschew thy fingers and the naughtiness thereof – get off – yea verily shall the Lord see that thou hast indeed been sore tempted but have from this day forward ceased to sin." And Brian eschewed his fingers and the use thereof for evermore, apart from odd occasions, and he was from that day forward blest in the sight of the Lord, and his name was called Saint Brian, and he dwelt amongst the Heavenly Host from that day forward.

MR CREOSOTE

MAÎTRE D: Ah good afternoon, sir, and how are we today?

MR CREOSOTE: Better . . .

MAÎTRE D: Better?

MR CREOSOTE: Better get a bucket, I'm going to throw up.

MAÎTRE D: Gaston! A bucket for monsieur!

They seat him at his usual table. A gleaming silver bucket is placed beside him and he leans over and throws up into it.

MAÎTRE D: Merci Gaston.

He claps his hands and the bucket is whisked away.

MR CREOSOTE: I haven't finished!

MAÎTRE D: Oh! Pardon! Gaston! . . . A thousand pardons monsieur. *(He puts the bucket back)*

The MAÎTRE D *produces the menu as* MR CREOSOTE *continues spewing.*

MAÎTRE D: Now this afternoon we have monsieur's favourite – the jugged hare. The hare is *very* high, and the sauce is very rich with truffles, anchovies, Grand Marnier, bacon and cream.

MR CREOSOTE *pauses. The* MAÎTRE D *claps his hands and signs to* GASTON*, who whisks away the bucket.*

MAÎTRE D: Thank you, Gaston.

MR CREOSOTE: There's still more.

GASTON *rapidly replaces the bucket.*

MAÎTRE D: Allow me! A new bucket for monsieur.

The MAÎTRE D *picks the bucket up and hands it over to* GASTON.

MR CREOSOTE *leans over and throws up on to the floor.*

And maintenant, would monsieur care for an apéritif?

MR CREOSOTE *vomits over the menu.*

Or would you prefer to order straight away? Today we have for appetizers . . . er . . . excuse me . . .

MAÎTRE D: . . . moules marinières, pâté de foie gras, beluga caviar, eggs Benedictine, tarte de poireaux – that's leek tart – frogs' legs amandine or oeufs de caille Richard Shepherd – c'est à dire, little quails' eggs on a bed of puréed mushrooms, it's very delicate, very subtle . . .

MR CREOSOTE: I'll have the lot.

MAÎTRE D: A wise choice, monsieur! And now, how would you like it served? All mixed up in a bucket?

MR CREOSOTE: Yes. With the eggs on top.

MAÎTRE D: But of course, avec les oeufs frites.

MR CREOSOTE: And don't skimp on the pâté.

MAÎTRE D: Oh monsieur I can assure you, just because it is mixed up with all the other things we would not dream of giving you less than the full amount. In fact I will personally make sure you have a *double* helping. Maintenant quelque chose à boire – something to drink, monsieur?

MR CREOSOTE: Yeah, six bottles of Château Latour '45 and a double Jeroboam of champagne.

MAÎTRE D: Bon, and the usual brown ales . . .?

MR CREOSOTE: Yeah . . . No wait a minute . . . I think I could only manage six crates today.

MAÎTRE D: Tut tut tut! I hope monsieur was not overdoing it last night . . .?

MR CREOSOTE: Shut up!

MAÎTRE D: D'accord. Ah the new bucket and the cleaning woman.

GASTON *arrives. The* CLEANING WOMAN *gets down on her hands and knees.* MR CREOSOTE *vomits over her.*

Some guests at another table start to leave. The MAÎTRE D
approaches.

MAÎTRE D: Monsieur, is there something wrong with the food?

The MAÎTRE D *indicates the table of half-eaten main courses. The
guests shrink from his vomit-covered hand. The* MAÎTRE D *realises and
shakes a little off. It hits another guest, who wipes his eye.*

GUEST: No. The food was . . . excellent . . .

They start to go. The MAÎTRE D *follows.*

MAÎTRE D: Thank you so much, so nice to see you and I hope very
much we will see you again very soon. Au revoir, monsieur.

He pauses. A look of awful realization suffuses his face.

MAÎTRE D: . . . Oh dear . . . I've trodden in monsieur's bucket.

The MAÎTRE D *claps his hands.*

Another bucket for monsieur . . .

MR CREOSOTE *is sick down the* MAÎTRE D*'s trousers.*

and perhaps a hose . . .

Someone at another table gently throws up.

COMPANION: Oh Max, really!

Meanwhile MR CREOSOTE *has scoffed the lot. The* MAÎTRE D *approaches
him with a silver tray.*

MAÎTRE D: And finally, monsieur, a wafer-thin mint.

MR CREOSOTE: No.

MAÎTRE D: Oh sir! It's only a tiny little one.

MR CREOSOTE: No. Fuck off – I'm full . . . *(Belches)*

MAÎTRE D: Oh sir . . . it's only *wafer* thin.

MR CREOSOTE: Look – I couldn't eat another thing. I'm absolutely
stuffed. Bugger off.

MAÎTRE D: Oh sir, just . . . just *one* . . .

MR CREOSOTE: Oh all right. Just one.

MAÎTRE D: Just the one, sir . . . voilà . . . bon appétit . . .

MR CREOSOTE *somehow manages to stuff the wafer-thin mint into his mouth and then swallows. The* MAÎTRE D *takes a flying leap and cowers behind some potted plants. There is an ominous splitting sound.* MR CREOSOTE *looks rather helpless and then he explodes.*

$TOCK
MARKET REPORT

Trading was crisp at the start of the day with some brisk business on the floor. Rubber hardened and string remained confident. Little bits of tin consolidated although biscuits sank after an early gain and stools remained anonymous. Armpits rallied well after a poor start. Nipples rose dramatically during the morning but had declined by mid-afternoon, while teeth clenched and buttocks remained firm. Small dark furry things increased severely on the floor, whilst rude jellies wobbled up and down, and bounced against rising thighs which had spread to all parts of the country by mid-afternoon. After lunch naughty things dipped sharply, forcing giblets upwards. Ting tang tong rankled dithely, little tipples pooped and poppy things went pong!

NOVEL WRITING
LIVE FROM DORCHESTER

COMMENTATOR: Hello and welcome to Dorchester where a very good crowd has turned out to watch local boy Thomas Hardy write his new novel, *The Return of the Native*, on this very pleasant July morning. And here he comes!

Here comes Hardy walking out towards his desk. He looks confident, he looks relaxed, very much the man in form, as he acknowledges this very good-natured bank holiday crowd . . .

And the crowd goes quiet now as Hardy settles himself down at the desk. Body straight . . . shoulders relaxed . . . pen held lightly but firmly in the right hand . . . the second finger coming round just underneath the base of the pen . . . he dips the pen in the ink . . . And he's off! And it's the first word! But it's not a word! Oh no! It's a doodle way up on the top of the left hand margin. It's a piece of meaningless scribble . . . and he's signed his name underneath it, oh dear, what a disappointing start . . . But he's off again! Yes there he goes – the first word of Thomas Hardy's new novel at 10.35 on this very lovely morning – it's three letters, it's the definite article and it's "The" . . . Richie Benaud.

RICHIE: Well this is true to form. No surprise there. He's started five of his eleven novels to date with the definite article, we've had two of them with "It", there's been one "But", two "Ats" and one "On" and a "Dolores", though that, of course, was never published.

COMMENTATOR: I'm sorry to interrupt you there, Richie, but he's crossed it out. Thomas Hardy here on the first day of his new novel has crossed out the only word he's written so far, and he's gazing off into space . . . But no, he's off and writing again . . . and yes: he's written "The" again! He's crossed it out again! That's twice he's written the definite article and twice he's crossed it out! And what's the replacement? It's . . . the indefinite article! This great novelist has replaced the definite article with the indefinite article, and there's a second word coming up straight away . . . no pause for thought . . . and it's "Sat" . . .

"A Sat . . ." doesn't make sense . . . "A Satur . . ." "A Saturday"! it's "A Saturday" and the crowd are loving it! They're really enjoying this novel. And it's "afternoon" . . . "A Saturday afternoon" . . . It's a confident beginning . . . And he's straight on to the next word . . . it's "in" . . . "A Saturday afternoon in . . . in . . . in . . . in . . . Novembr!" November spelt wrong . . . he's left out the second "e" . . . but he's not going back! It looks as though he's going to go for the sentence! And it's the first verb coming up! It's the first verb of the novel . . . and it's "was"! And the crowd are going wild! "A Saturday afternoon in November was . . ." and a long word here . . . "appro . . ." is it "approval"? No! It's "approaching"! "A Saturday afternoon in November was approaching" and he's done the definite article, "the", again, and he's writing fluently, easily, with flowing strokes of his pen, as he comes up to the middle of this first sentence . . . and with this eleventh novel well under way and the prospects of a good day's writing ahead, back to the studio.

THE KNIGHTS WHO SAY
'NI'

Big close-up of a frightening black-browed evil face.

TALL KNIGHT: Ni!

KING ARTHUR *and* SIR BEDEVERE *recoil in abject fear.* PATSY *rears up with coconuts.*

ARTHUR: Easy . . . boy, easy . . .

(He peers into the darkness.)

Who are you?

SIX VOICES FROM THE DARKNESS: Ni! . . . Peng! . . . Neeee . . . Wom!

An extraordinarily TALL KNIGHT *all in black looms out of the darkness. He is extremely fierce and of gruesome countenance.*

ARTHUR: Who are you?

TALL KNIGHT: We are the Knights Who Say "Ni"!

BEDEVERE *(in terror)*: No! Not the Knights Who Say "Ni"!

TALL KNIGHT: The same . . .

ARTHUR: Who are they?

TALL KNIGHT: We are the keepers of the Sacred Words. Ni . . . Peng . . . and Neee . . . Wom!

BEDEVERE: Those who hear them seldom live to tell the tale.

TALL KNIGHT: The Knights Who Say "Ni"! demand a sacrifice.

ARTHUR: Knights Who Say "Ni" . . . we are but simple travellers. We seek the Enchanter who lives beyond this wood and who . . .

TALL KNIGHT: Ni!

ARTHUR *(recoiling)*: Oh!

TALL KNIGHT: Ni! Ni!

ARTHUR *(he cowers in fear)*: Oh!

TALL KNIGHT: We shall say "Ni!" again if you do not appease us.

ARTHUR: All right! What do you want?

TALL KNIGHT: We want . . . a shrubbery!

ARTHUR: A *what*?

TALL KNIGHT: Ni! Ni! Ni . . . Peng . . . Nee . . . wom!

The PAGES *rear and snort and rattle their coconuts.*

ARTHUR: All right! All right! . . . no more, please. We will find you a shrubbery . . .

TALL KNIGHT: You must return here with a shrubbery or else . . . you shall not pass through this wood alive!

ARTHUR: Thank you, Knights Who Say Ni! You are fair and just. We will return with a shrubbery.

TALL KNIGHT: One that looks nice.

192

ARTHUR: Of course.

TALL KNIGHT: And not too expensive.

ARTHUR: Yes . . .

TALL KNIGHT: Now – go!

ARTHUR *and* BEDEVERE *turn and ride off. Shouts of* "Ni" *and* "Peng" *ring behind them.*

August 5th, 1974.

Dear Mike,

The Censor's representative, Tony Kerpel, came along to Friday's screening at Twickenham and he gave us his opinion of the film's probable certificate.

He thinks the film will be AA, but it would be possible, given some dialogue cuts, to make the film an A rating, which would increase the audience. (AA is 14 and over, and A is 5 — 14).

For an "A" we would have to:

Lose as many *shits* as possible
Take *Jesus Christ* out, if possible
Lose "I fart in your general direction"
Lose "the *oral sex*"
Lose "oh, *fuck off*"
Lose "We make castanets out of your testicles"

I would like to get back to the Censor and agree to lose the *shits*, take the odd *Jesus Christ* out and lose *Oh fuck off*, but to retain "fart in your general direction", "castanets of your testicles" and "oral sex" and ask him for an "A" rating on that basis.

Please let me know as soon as possible your attitude to this.

Yours sincerely

Mark Forstater

SELECTED
BY
TERRY
JONES

WITH A PREFACE BY TERRY GILLIAM

A PREFACE BY THE
OTHER TERRY

Terry Jones is a sack of stories. A great wobbly sack like the one Father Christmas bundles around on his back, but full of wondrous smelly things, plump pictures, foolish, outrageous and naughty creatures, tumescent vicars.

He's always seemed round to me. When I first met Terry he wasn't physically round as he has become (beware the Ides of Creosote) - but 'round' always seemed to describe him. His insatiable appetite for life and food and wine and sex and passionately held beliefs has always seemed to demand a big round container in which to stockpile them.

Luckily for Terry, this container has many interesting orifices to provide entrance and egress for life's little pleasures - and the massive amounts of material that interest him. Terry has always shared them with us - not the orifices, but the material.

Sometimes the stuff coming out is just hot air and noxious gasses but more often it is stories and tales, histories and myths, dreams and fabulous worlds, serious and important ideas. These marvels have all managed to find an exit point before Terry's internal pressure gauge reached danger levels.

Thank God! I would hesitate to imagine the mess if they hadn't.

TG May 1999

INTRODUCTION

What I remember most about the making of Monty Python is the curry. We would sit together and plan the shows over a *rhogan josh* and a bit of *dal*, and then go our separate ways to try out the *raita*, the *sag aloo* and the *onion bhajees*, before getting back together again for a *lamb masala*, *prawn biryani*, *meat dopiaza* and a *chicken chat*. Sometimes the curries lasted until the early hours of the morning. We'd all be there - Graham, John, Mike, Terry G and Eric, battling to put away the last of the *patia* or the final bit of *korma*, knowing that by the morning the BBC would expect us to have a complete vegetarian *thali* assembled or at the least a working outline of a decent *bhuna gosht* or a cracking *vindaloo* with plenty of *shaslick* and *oree bhaji* on the side! My goodness, how we fought the BBC Light Entertainment bosses over our right to include *kaboli mutter* and *aloo zeera* as genuine recipes, and how we battled over the *mutter paneer* and the *chana mossala* that they claimed would never be tolerated by our customers in the more provincial cities.

But we showed 'em. We proved that a decent standard of vegetable curry is as acceptable to the majority of people as a *chicken jalfriizi* or a *king prawn dansak*.

So when I was asked to put together this selection of my favourite texts from the Monty Python books, shows and films, I naturally went for the one that expressed the true essence of Python - the curries. I deliberately avoided any sketches or extracts that did not include at least one or more of the following words: "tandoori", "balti", "Ceylon", "pasanda", "paratha", "bindi" or "brinjal bhaji".

I apologize if readers feel this has constrained my choice unnecessarily, but I believe it is better to include less, but more essentially Pythonic, material than just anything that made me laugh.

So "peshwari nan" to you all and I hope you enjoy this Punjabi feast of fun.

TJ April 1999

THE FRENCH TAUNT KING ARTHUR

You don't frighten us, English pig-dog. Go and boil your bottom, son of a silly person. I blow my nose on you so-called Arthur King, you and your silly English k....niggetsI don't want to talk to you no more, you empty- headed animal food trough wiper. I fart in your general direction. Your mother was a hamster and your father smelled of elderberries.

THE TRUTH ABOUT PROTESTANTS

MR BLACKITT: Look at them, bloody Catholics. Filling the bloody world up with bloody people they can't afford to bloody feed.

MRS BLACKITT: What are we dear?

MR BLACKITT: Protestants, and fiercely proud of it....

MRS BLACKITT: Why do they have so many children....?

MR BLACKITT: Because every time they have sexual intercourse they have to have a baby.

MRS BLACKITT: But it's the same with us, Harry.

MR BLACKITT: What d'you mean...?

MRS BLACKITT: Well I mean we've got two children and we've had sexual intercourse twice.

MR BLACKITT: That's not the point.... We could have it any time we wanted.

MRS BLACKITT: Really?

MR BLACKITT: Oh yes. And, what's more, because we don't believe in all that Papist claptrap we can take precautions.

MRS BLACKITT: What, you mean lock the door...?

MR BLACKITT: No, no. I mean because we are members of the Protestant Reformed Church which successfully challenged the autocratic power of the Papacy in the mid-sixteenth century we can wear little rubber devices to prevent issue.

MRS BLACKITT: What do you mean?

MR BLACKITT: I could, if I wanted, have sexual intercourse with you...

MRS BLACKITT: Oh, yes...Harry....

MR BLACKITT: And by wearing a rubber sheath over my old feller I could ensure that when I came off...you would not be impregnated.

MRS BLACKITT: Ooh!

MR BLACKITT: That's what being a Protestant's all about. That's why it's the church for me. That's why it's the church for anyone who respects the individual and the individual's right to decide for him or herself. When Martin Luther nailed his protest up to the church door in 1517, he may not have realised the full significance of what he was doing. But four hundred years later, thanks to him, my dear, I can wear whatever I want on my John Thomas. And Protestantism doesn't stop at the simple condom. Oh no! I can wear French Ticklers if I want.

MRS BLACKITT: You what?

MR BLACKITT: French Ticklers, Black Mambos, Crocodile Ribs...Sheaths that are designed not only to protect but also to enhance the stimulation of sexual congress....

MRS BLACKITT: Have you got one?

MR BLACKITT: Have I got one? Well no... But I can go down the road any time I want and walk into Harry's and hold my head up high, and say in a loud steady voice: 'Harry I want you to sell me a condom. In fact today I think I'll have a French Tickler, for I am a Protestant....'

MRS BLACKITT: Well why don't you?

MR BLACKITT: But they...they cannot. Because their church never made the great leap out of the Middle Ages, and the domination of alien episcopal supremacy.

THE LUMBERJACK
SONG

BARBER: I didn't want to be a barber anyway. I wanted to be a lumberjack. Leaping from tree to tree as they float down the mighty rivers of British Columbia... The giant redwood, the larch, the fir, the mighty scots pine. *(a choir of Mounties is heard faintly in the distance)* The smell of fresh-cut timber! The crash of mighty trees! With my best girlie by my side... We'd sing...sing...sing.

I'm a lumberjack and I'm OK,
I sleep all night and I work all day.
MOUNTIES CHOIR: He's a lumberjack and he's OK,
He sleeps all night and he works all day.
BARBER: I cut down trees, I eat my lunch,
I go to the lavatory.
On Wednesdays I go shopping,
And have buttered scones for tea.

MOUNTIES CHOIR: He cuts down trees, he eats his lunch,
He goes to the lavatory.
On Wednesdays he goes shopping,
And has buttered scones for tea.
He's a lumberjack and he's OK,
He sleeps all night and he works all day.

BARBER: I cut down trees, I skip and jump,
I like to press wild flowers,
I put on women's clothing
And hang around in bars.

MOUNTIES CHOIR: He cuts down trees,
he skips and jumps,
He likes to press wild flowers.
He puts on women's clothing
And hangs around in bars...?
He's a lumberjack and he's OK,
He sleeps all night and he works all day.

BARBER: I cut down trees, I wear high heels,
Suspenders and a bra.
I wish I'd been a girlie,
Just like my dear Mama.
MOUNTIES CHOIR: He cuts down trees,
he wears high heels,
Suspenders...and a bra?...

GIRL: Oh Bevis! And I thought
you were so rugged.

THE **PRODIGAL SON**
RETURNS

A sitting room straight out of D.H. Lawrence. Mum, wiping her hands on her arm and ushering in a young man in a suit.

MUM: Oh Dad...look who's come to see us...it's our Ken.

DAD *(without looking up)*: Aye, and about bloody time if you ask me.

KEN: Aren't you pleased to see me, Father?

MUM *(squeezing his arm reassuringly)*: Of course he's pleased to see you, Ken, he...

DAD: All right, woman, all right I've got a tongue in my head - I'll do t'talkin' *(looks at Ken distastefully)* Aye...I like yer fancy suit. Is that what their wearing up in Yorkshire now?

KEN: It's just an ordinary suit, father...it's all I've got apart from the overalls.

Dad turns away with an expression of scornful disgust.

MUM: How are you liking it down the mine, Ken?

KEN: Oh, it's not too bad, mum...we're using some new tungsten carbide drills for the preliminary coal-face scouring operations.

MUM: Oh that sounds nice, dear...

DAD: Tungsten carbide drills! What the bloody hell's tungsten carbide drills?

KEN: It's something they use in coal-mining, Father.

DAD *(mimicking)*: 'It's something they use in coal-mining, father'. You're all bloody fancy talk since you left London.

KEN: Oh not that again.

MUM *(to Ken)*: He's had a hard day dear...his new play opens at the National Theatre tomorrow.

KEN: Oh that's good.

DAD: Good! *good?* What do you know about it? What do you know about getting up at five o'clock in t'morning to fly to Paris...back at the Old Vic for drinks at twelve, sweating the day through press interviews, television interviews and getting back here at ten to wrestle with the problem of a homosexual nymphomaniac drug-addict involved in the ritual murder of a well known Scottish foot-baller. That's a full working day, lad, and don't you forget it!

MUM: Oh, don't shout at the boy, Father.

DAD: Aye, 'ampstead wasn't good enough for you, was it?...you had to go poncing off to Barnsley, you and yer coal-mining friends. *(spits)*

KEN: Coal-mining is a wonderful thing, Father, but it's something you'll never understand. Just look at you!

MUM: Oh Ken! Be careful! You know what he's like after a few novels.

DAD: Oh come on lad! Come on, out wi' it! What's wrong wi' me?...you *tit*!

KEN: I'll tell you what's wrong with you. Your head's addled with novels and poems, you come home every evening reeking of Château La Tour...

MUM: Oh don't, don't.

KEN: And look what you've done to mother! She's worn out with meeting film stars, attending premières and giving gala luncheons...

DAD: There's nowt wrong wi' gala luncheons, lad! I've had more gala luncheons than you've had hot dinners!

MUM: Oh please!

DAD: Aaaaaaagh! *(clutches hands and sinks to knees)*

MUM: Oh no!

KEN: What is it?

MUM: Oh, it's his writer's cramp!

KEN: You never told me about this...

MUM: No, we didn't like to, Kenny.

DAD: I'm all right! I'm all right, woman. Just get him out of here.

KEN: All right. I'm going.

DAD: After all we've done for him...

KEN *(at the door)*: One day you'll realize there's more to life than culture...There's dirt, and smoke, and good honest sweat!

DAD: Get out! Get out! Get OUT! You...LABOURER!

Ken goes. Shocked silence. Dad goes to table and takes the cover off the typewriter.

DAD: Hey, you know, mother, I think there's a play there...get t'agent on t'phone.

MUM: Aye I think you're right, Frank, it could express, it could express a vital theme of our age...

DAD: Aye.

THE NEWS FOR PARROTS

Good evening. Here is the News for parrots. No parrots were involved in an accident on the M1 today, when a lorry carrying high octane fuel was in collision with a bollard...that is a *bollard* and not a *parrot*. A spokesman for parrots said he was glad no parrots were involved. The Minister of Technology today met the three Russian leaders to discuss a £4 million airliner deal... None of them went in the cage, or swung on the little wooden trapeze, or ate any of the nice millet seed, yum, yum. That's the end of the news. Now our programmes for parrots continue with part three of "A Tale of Two Cities" specially adapted for parrots by Joey Boy. The story so far...Dr Manette is in England after eighteen years in the Bastille. His daughter Lucy awaits her lover Charles Darnay who, we have just learned, is in fact the nephew of the Marquis de St Evremond, whose cruelty had placed Manette in the Bastille. Darnay arrives to find Lucy tending her aged father...

London 1793. An eighteenth-century living room. Lucy is nursing her father. Suddenly the door bursts open and Charles Darnay enters.

DARNAY: 'Allo, 'allo.
LUCY: 'Allo, 'allo, 'allo.
OLD MAN: 'Allo, 'allo, 'allo.
DARNAY: Who's a pretty boy then?

RAT PIE

Take four medium-sized rats and lay them on the chopping board.
Having first made sure the chopper is freshly sharpened, raise it as
high above the first rat as you can. Make sure that the rat's neck is
well exposed, then bring the chopper down with as much force as
possible onto the neck or head of the rat. Then cook it in a pie.

RAT SOUFFLÉ

Make sure that the rat's squeals are not audible from the street, particularly in areas where the Anti-Soufflé League and similar do-
gooders are out to persecute the innocent pleasures of the table.
Anyway, cut the rat down and lay it on the chopping board.
Raise the chopper high above your head, with the steel glinting in
the setting sun, and then bring it down - wham! - with a vivid crunch -
straight across the taut neck of the terrified rodent, and make it into
a soufflé.

Bits of rat hidden under a chair:
This isn't so much a recipe as a bit of advice in the event of members of the Anti-Soufflé League or its simpering lackeys breaking into your flat. Your wife (or a friend's) should engage the pusillanimous toadies from the League in conversation, perhaps turning the chat to the price of corn and the terrible damage inflicted by all kinds of rodents on personal property, and rats attacking small babies (this bit always takes the steam out of them) and you should have time to get any rat-bits safely out of sight. Incidentally, do make sure that your current copy of *The Rat Gourmet* hasn't been left lying around, otherwise all will be in vain, and the braying hounds of the culinary killjoys will be unleashed upon the things you cherish: your chopping board, the chopper caught in the blood-red glare of the fading sun. Bring it down - crunch! The slight splintering of the tiny spinal column under the keen metal! The last squeal and the death twitches of the helpless rat!

WHAT HAVE THE ROMANS EVER DONE FOR US?

The interior of Matthias's house. A cellar-like room with a very conspiratorial atmosphere.

REG: They've bled us white, the bastards. They've taken everything we had, not just from us, from our fathers and from our fathers' fathers.

STAN: And from our fathers' fathers' fathers.

REG: Yes.

STAN: And our fathers' fathers' fathers' fathers.

REG: All right, Stan. Don't labour the point. And what have they ever given us in return?

He pauses smugly.

Voice from masked commando.

XERXES: The aqueduct?

REG: What?

XERXES: The aqueduct.

REG: Oh yeah, yeah, they gave us that. Yeah. That's true.

MASKED COMMANDO: And the sanitation!

STAN: Oh yes...sanitation, Reg, you remember what the city used to be like.

Murmurs of agreement.

REG: All right, I'll grant you that the aqueduct and the sanitation are two things that the Romans have done...

MATTHIAS: And the roads...

REG *(sharply)*: Well yes obviously the roads..the roads go without saying. But apart from the aqueduct, the sanitation and the roads...

ANOTHER MASKED COMMANDO: Irrigation...

OTHER MASKED VOICES: Medicine...Education...Health.

REG: Yes...all right, fair enough...

COMMANDO NEARER THE FRONT: And the wine...

GENERAL: Oh yes! True?

FRANCIS: Yeah. That's something we'd really miss if the Romans left, Reg.

MASKED COMMANDO AT BACK: Public baths!

STAN: And it's safe to walk in the streets at night now.

FRANCIS: Yes, they certainly know how to keep order...

General nodding.

...let's face it, they're the only ones who could in a place like this.

More general murmurs of agreement.

REG: All right...all right...but apart from better sanitation and medicine and education and irrigation and public health and roads and a freshwater system and baths and public order...what have the Romans done for us...?

XERXES: Brought peace!

REG *(very angry, he's not having a good meeting at all)*: What!? Oh...*(scornfully)* Peace, yes...shut up!

A PAGE FOR THOSE WHO LIKE FIGURES OF SPEECH

This is a page specially written for people who like figures of speech, for the not a few fans of litotes and those with no small interest in meiosis, for the infinite millions of hyperbole-lovers, for those fond of hypallage and the epithet's golden transfer, for those who fall willingly into the arms of the metaphor, those who give up the ghost, bury their heads in the sand and ride roughshod over the mixed metaphor, and even those of hyperbaton the friends. It will be too, for those who reprehend the malapropism; who love the wealth of metonymy; for all friends of rhetoric and syllepsis; and zeugmatists with smiling eyes and hearts. It will bring a large absence of unsatisfactory malevolence to periphrastic fans; a wig harm bello to spoonerists; and in no small measure a not less than splendid greeting to you circumlocutors. The World adores prosopopeiasts, and the friendly faces of synechdochists, and can one not make those amorous of anacoluthon understand that if they are not satisfied by this, what is to happen to them? It will attempt to really welcome all splitters of infinitives, all who are Romeo and Juliet to antonomasia, those who drink up similes like sparkling champagne, who lose nothing compared with comparison heads, self-evident axiomists, all pithy aphorists, apothegemists, maximiles, theorists, epigrammatists and even gnomists. And as for the lovers of aposiopeses...! It will wish bienvenu to all classical adherents of euphuism, all metathesistic birds, golden paronomasiasts covered in guilt, fallacious paralogists, trophists, anagogists, and anaphorists; to greet, welcome, embrace asyndeton buffs, while the lovers of ellipsis will be well-met and its followers embraced, as will be chronic worshippers of catachresis and supporters of anastrophe the world over.

FIND THE FISH

LADY TV PRESENTER: Hallo and welcome to the Middle Of The Film. The moment where we take a break and invite you, the audience, to join us, the film-makers, in "Find The Fish". We're going to show you a scene from another film and ask you to guess where the fish is. But if you think you know, don't keep it to yourselves - YELL OUT - so that all the cinema can hear you. So here we are with "Find The Fish".

MAN: I wonder where that fish has gone.
WOMAN: You did love it so.
You looked after it like a son.
MAN *(strangely):* And it went wherever I did go.
WOMAN: Is it in the cupboard?
AUDIENCE: Yes! No!
WOMAN: Wouldn't you like to know.
It was a lovely little fish.
MAN *(strangely):* And it went wherever I did go.
MAN IN AUDIENCE: It's behind the sofa!
An elephant joins the man and the woman.
WOMAN: Where can the fish be?
MAN IN AUDIENCE: Have you thought of the drawers in the bureau?
WOMAN: It is a most elusive fish.
MAN *(strangely):* And it went wherever I did go!
WOMAN: Oh fishy, fishy, fishy, fish.
MAN: Fish, fish, fish fishy oh!
WOMAN: Oh fishy, fishy, fishy, fish.
MAN *(strangely):* That went wherever I did go.

ALBATROSS

A man in an ice-cream girl's uniform is standing in a spotlight with an ice-cream tray with an albatross on it.

MAN: Albatross! Albatross! Albatross!
A person approaches him.
PERSON: Two choc-ices please.
MAN: I haven't got choc-ices. I only got the albatross. Albatross!
PERSON: What flavour is it?
MAN: It's a bird, innit. It's a bloody sea bird...it's not any bloody flavour. Albatross!
PERSON: Do you get wafers with it?
MAN: 'Course you don't get bloody wafers with it. Albatross!
PERSON: How much is it?
MAN: Ninepence.
PERSON: I'll have two please.
MAN: Gannet on a stick.

OUR THEATRE CRITIC REVIEWS

THE MERCHANT OF VENICE

**PERFORMED BY THE DAIRY
HERD OF BAD TOLTZ**

It is always a joy to welcome a new interpretation of one of Shakespeare's works, but seldom do we find something so totally and refreshingly original as this production by the cows of Bad Toltz.

The Merchant of Venice has always been a difficult play for animals. I remember some chickens from Kaiserslauten having a shot at it three years ago, and failing miserably. But these cows have avoided all the pitfalls that the chickens fell into. They haven't tried to dress up, they haven't tried to make the play into an allegory about eggs, and they don't run away all the time. I loved it. And I can't wait to see these fine dairy cows get to grips with Wagner at Bayreuth next week.

MADAME PALM WRITES AGAIN

Dear Madame Palm,
Our Local Building Society
Branch Manager says that Insur-
ance is illegal. Can this be true?
Ron Higgins, Cirencester.

Dear Ron, there is absolutely no need to be ashamed of your body. Sex is a perfectly natural function that all post-pubescent people indulge in. For heavens sake can't we get it out in the open?

Dear Madame Palm,
What can I do about acne? I
have tried everything, creams,
jellies, injections, pumice stone,
dieting, tablets and mud packs,
but no matter what I do my skin
remains smooth and clear. Can
you buy acne?
Yours hopefully,
R. Bradshaw, Biggleswade.

Dear R. Bradshaw, please believe me when I tell you that sex is absolutely normal for people of all ages and between everybody and anyone except filthy perverts who should be castrated and locked away for ever, honestly, hanging is too good for them. Love and understanding will go a long way towards curing all the ills in the world except nasty filthy perverts who should be put down at once.

Dear Madame Palm,
Can you settle a family argu-
ment? My parents say that black
and white television is really in
colour, but I maintain that colour
TV is really black and white. Who
is right?
Puzzled, Wakefield.

Dear Puzzled, sex is one of God's greatest gifts, along with nudity, golf and wrestling. Please try and understand that no matter how dirty your desires may seem they are perfectly natural.
P.S. I am sending you some leaflets. Good aren't they?

SPAM

*A café. All the customers are Vikings. Mr and Mrs Bun
enter - downwards.*

MR BUN: Morning.
WAITRESS: Morning.
MR BUN: What have you got, then?
WAITRESS: Well there's egg and bacon; egg, sausage and bacon; egg
and spam; egg, bacon and spam; egg, bacon, sausage and spam;
spam, bacon sausage and spam; spam, egg, spam, spam, bacon and
spam; spam, spam, spam, egg and spam; spam, spam, spam, spam,
spam, spam, baked beans, spam, spam, spam, and spam; or lobster
thermidor aux crevettes with a mornay sauce garnished with truffle
pâté, brandy and a fried egg on top and spam.
MRS BUN: Have you got anything without spam in it?
WAITRESS: Well, there's spam, egg, sausage and spam. That's not got
much spam in it.
MRS BUN: I don't want *any* spam.
MR BUN: Why can't she have egg, bacon spam and sausage?
MRS BUN: That's got spam in it!
MR BUN: Not as much as spam, egg, sausage and spam.
MRS BUN: Look, could I have egg, bacon, spam and sausage without
the spam.
WAITRESS: Uuuuuugggggh!
MRS BUN: What d'you mean uuugggh! I don't like spam.
VIKINGS *(singing)*: Spam, spam, spam, spam, spam...spam, spam,
spam, spam...lovely spam, wonderful spam...
WAITRESS: Shut up. Shut up! Shut up! You can't have egg, bacon, spam
and sausage without the spam.
MRS BUN: Why not?

WAITRESS: No, it wouldn't be egg, bacon, spam and sausage, would it.

MRS BUN: I don't like spam!

MR BUN: Don't make a fuss, dear. I'll have your spam. I love it. I'm having spam, spam, spam, spam, spam...

VIKINGS *(singing)*: Spam, spam, spam, spam...

MR BUN: ...baked beans, spam, spam and spam.

WAITRESS: Baked beans are off.

MR BUN: Well can I have spam instead?

WAITRESS: You mean spam, spam, spam, spam, spam, spam, spam, spam, spam, spam?

VIKINGS *(still singing)*: Spam, spam, spam, spam...

MR BUN: Yes.

WAITRESS: Arrggh!

VIKINGS: ...lovely spam, wonderful, spam.

WAITRESS: Shut up! Shut up!

Superimposed caption: "A Historian"

HISTORIAN: Another great Viking victory was at the Green Midget café at Bromley. Once again the Viking strategy was the same. They sailed from these fiords here *(indicating a map with arrows on it)*, assembled at Trondheim and waited for the strong north-easterly winds to blow their oaken galleys to England whence they sailed on May 23rd. Once in Bromley they assembled in the Green Midget café and spam selecting a spam particular spam item from the spam menu would spam, spam, spam, spam, spam...

The backdrop behind him rises to reveal the café again. The Vikings start singing again and the historian conducts them.

VIKINGS *(singing)*: Spam, spam, spam, spam, spam, lovely spam, wonderful spam. Lovely spam, wonderful spam...

CONSTITUTIONAL
PEASANTS

KING ARTHUR *and his squire* PATSY *overtake a* PEASANT *pulling a cart towards a distant castle.*

ARTHUR: Old woman!

DENNIS: *(turning)*: Man.

ARTHUR: Man. I'm sorry. Old man, what knight lives in that castle?

DENNIS: I'm thirty-seven.

ARTHUR: What?

DENNIS: I'm only thirty-seven...I'm not old.

ARTHUR: Well - I can't just say: "Hey, Man!"

DENNIS: You could say: "Dennis".

ARTHUR: I didn't know you were called Dennis.

DENNIS: You didn't bother to find out, did you?

ARTHUR: I've said I'm sorry about the old woman, but from behind you looked...

DENNIS: What I object to is that you automatically treat me as an inferior...

ARTHUR: Well...I am King.

DENNIS: Oh, very nice. King, eh! I expect you've got a palace and fine clothes and courtiers and plenty of food. And how d'you get that? By exploiting the workers! By hanging onto outdated imperialistic dogma, which perpetuates the social and economic differences in our society! If there's ever going to be any progress...

An OLD WOMAN *appears.*

OLD WOMAN: Dennis! There's some lovely filth down here...Oh! How d'you do?

ARTHUR: How d'you do, good lady...I am Arthur, King of the Britons...can you tell me who lives in that castle?

OLD WOMAN: King of the who?

ARTHUR: The Britons.

OLD WOMAN: Who are the Britons?

ARTHUR: All of us are...we are all Britons. (DENNIS *winks at the* OLD

228

WOMAN)...And I am your King...

OLD WOMAN: Ooooh! I didn't know we had a king. I thought we were an autonomous collective...

DENNIS: You're fooling yourself. We're living in a dictatorship, a self-perpetuating autocracy in which the working classes...

OLD WOMAN: There you are, bringing class into it again...

DENNIS: That's what it's all about...If only...

ARTHUR: Please, please, good people, I am in haste. What knight lives in that castle?

OLD WOMAN: No one lives there.

ARTHUR: Well, who is your lord?

OLD WOMAN: We don't have a lord.

ARTHUR: What?

DENNIS: I told you, we're an anarcho-syndicalist commune, we take it in turns to act as a sort of executive officer for the week.

ARTHUR: Yes...

DENNIS: ...But all the decisions of that officer...

ARTHUR: Yes, I see.

DENNIS: ...must be approved at a bi-weekly meeting by a simple majority in the case of purely internal affairs...

ARTHUR: Be quiet.

DENNIS: But a two-thirds majority...

ARTHUR: Be quiet! I order you to shut up.

OLD WOMAN: Order, eh? Who does he think he is?

ARTHUR: I am your King.

OLD WOMAN: Well, I didn't vote for you.

ARTHUR: You don't vote for kings.

OLD WOMAN: Well, how did you become King, then?

ARTHUR: The Lady of the Lake, her arm clad in purest shimmering samite, held Excalibur aloft from the bosom of the waters to signify that by Divine Providence...I, Arthur, was to carry Excalibur...that is why I am your King.

DENNIS: Look, strange women lying on their backs in ponds handing over swords...that's no basis for a system of government. Supreme executive power derives from a mandate from the masses not from some farcical aquatic ceremony.

ARTHUR: Be quiet!

DENNIS: You can't expect to wield supreme executive power just because some watery tart threw a sword at you.

ARTHUR: Shut up!

DENNIS: I mean, if I went around saying I was an Emperor because some moistened bint had lobbed a scimitar at me, people would put me away.

ARTHUR *(grabbing him by the collar)*: Shut up, will you. Shut up!

DENNIS: Ah! *Now*...we see the violence inherent in the system.

...EVERY SPERM IS SACRED

There are Jews in the world,
There are Buddhists,
There are Hindus and Mormons and then,
There are those that follow Mohammed,
But I've never been one of them...
I'm a Roman Catholic,
And have been since before I was born,
And the one thing they say about Catholics,
Is they'll take you as soon as you're warm...
You don't have to be a six-footer,
You don't have to have a great brain,
You don't have to have any clothes on
You're a Catholic the moment Dad came...
Because...

Every sperm is sacred,
Every sperm is great,
If a sperm is wasted,
God gets quite irate.

Let the heathen spill theirs,
On the dusty ground,
God shall make them pay for
Each sperm that can't be found.

Every sperm is wanted,
Every sperm is good,
Every sperm is needed
In your neighbourhood.

Hindu, Taoist, Mormon,
Spill theirs just anywhere,
But God loves those who treat their
Semen with more care.

Every sperm is sacred,
Every sperm is great,
If a sperm is wasted
God gets quite irate.

Every sperm is sacred,
Every sperm is good,
Every sperm is needed
In your neighbourhood.

Every sperm is useful,
Every sperm is fine,
God needs everybody's,
Mine!
And mine!
And mine!

Every sperm is sacred,
Every sperm is good,
Every sperm is needed
In your neighbourhood.

Let the pagan spill theirs,
O'er mountain, hill and plain,
God shall strike them down for
Each sperm that's spilt in vain.

Every sperm is sacred,
Every sperm is great,
If a sperm is wasted,
God gets quite irate.

THE UNDERTAKER
SKETCH

An undertaker's shop.

UNDERTAKER: Morning.

MAN: Good morning.

UNDERTAKER: What can I do for you, squire?

MAN: Well, I wonder if you can help me. You see, my mother has just died.

UNDERTAKER: Ah well, we can help you. We deal with stiffs.

MAN: What?

UNDERTAKER: Well, there's three things we can do with your mum. We can burn her, bury her or dump her.

MAN *(shocked)*: Dump her?

UNDERTAKER: Dump her in the Thames.

MAN: What?

UNDERTAKER: Oh, did you like her?

MAN: Yes!

UNDERTAKER: Oh well, we won't dump her, then. Well what do you think? We can bury her or burn her.

MAN: Well, which do you recommend?

UNDERTAKER: Well, they're both nasty. If we burn her she gets stuffed in the flames, crackle, crackle, crackle, which is a bit of a shock if she's not quite dead, but quick, and then we give you a handful of ashes, which you can pretend were hers.

MAN: Oh.

UNDERTAKER: Or if we bury her she gets eaten up by lots of weevils, and nasty maggots, which as I said before is a bit of a shock if she's not quite dead.

MAN: I see. Well, she's definitely dead.

UNDERTAKER: Where is she?

MAN: She's in this sack.

UNDERTAKER: Can I have a look? She looks quite young.

MAN: Yes, yes, she was.

UNDERTAKER *(calling)*: Fred!

FRED'S VOICE: Yeah?

UNDERTAKER: I think we've got an eater.

MAN: What?

Another undertaker pokes his head round the door.

FRED: Right, I'll get the oven on. *(He goes off)*

MAN: Er, excuse me, um, are you suggesting eating my mother?

UNDERTAKER: Er...yeah, not raw. Cooked.

MAN: What?

UNDERTAKER: Yes, roasted with a few french fries, broccoli, horseradish sauce...

MAN: Well, I do feel a bit peckish.

UNDERTAKER: Great!

MAN: Can we have some parsnips?

UNDERTAKER *(calling)*: Fred - get some parsnips.

MAN: I really don't think I should.

UNDERTAKER: Look, tell you what, we'll eat her; if you feel a bit guilty about it after, we can dig a grave and you can throw up in it.

MADAME PALM
WRITES YET AGAIN

Dear Sir or Madame Palm,
I, or rather a friend of mine, although I suppose I might as well be honest and say straight out that it is really me, but it may not be me. I could have a friend like it as well, but no! To be honest, it is me, suffer from indecision. Probably.

I have lost two or three or perhaps five jobs in the last day or days. Please tell me what to do. No, no, don't. Yours faithfully or sincerely, Stephen or Mavis Buchanan,or Jack Noonan.

Dear All, no of course you can't get pregnant that way.

Dear Madame Palm.
Our dog Nipper has just won a seat in the U.S. Senate. Will he have to be vaccinated? Yours, Y.Wilcox, Preston.

Yes Mr Wilcox, I'm afraid all U.S. Senators have to be vaccinated.

Dear Madame Palm,
I served for eight years with the Ghurkas. We fought against incredible odds in all parts of the North Western Frontier to safeguard the freedom and the right to self-determination of the people of Southern Asia. I am now a part-time notice board in a prominent public school. I also prefer wearing women's dresses. Are there anyother ex-Ghurkas similarly interested?NAME AND RANK SUPPLIED.

Dear Name and Rank Supplied, what a lovely name. No of course you shouldn't give up. Try taking a hot bath first to relax yourself and then keep trying. Don't worry if it doesn't work at first, it'll soon become fun and practice makes perfect, as the doctors say.
There's nothing better than a jolly good

THE **MAN** WHO TALKS ENTIRELY IN **ANAGRAMS**

INTERVIEWER: Hello, good evening and welcome to another edition of "Blood, Devastation, Death, War and Horror", and later on we'll be talking to a man who *does* gardening. But our first guest in the studio tonight is a man who talks entirely in anagrams.

MAN: Taht si crreoct.

INTERVIEWER: Do you enjoy this?

MAN: I stom certainly od. Revy chum so.

INTERVIEWER: And what's your name?

MAN: Hamrag. Hamrag Yatlerot.

INTERVIEWER: Well, Graham, nice to have you on the show. Now where do you come from?

MAN: Bumcreland.

INTERVIEWER: Cumberland?

MAN: Staht sit sepreicly.

INTERVIEWER: And I believe you're working on an anagram version of Shakespeare...

MAN: Sey, sey, taht si crreoct, er. Ta the mnemot I'm wroking on *The Mating of the Wersh*.

INTERVIEWER: *The Mating of the Wersh*. By William Shakespeare?

MAN: Nay, by Malliwi Rapesheake.

INTERVIEWER: And er, what else?

MAN: *Two Netlemeg of Verona*, *Twelfth Thing*, *The Chamrent of Venice*...

239

INTERVIEWER: Have you done *Hamlet*?

MAN: *Thamle*. "Be ot or bot ne ot, tath is the nestquie".

INTERVIEWER: And what is your next project?

MAN: *Ring Kichard the Thrid*

INTERVIEWER: I'm sorry?

MAN: "A shroe! A shroe! My dingkome for a shroe!"

INTERVIEWER: Ah, Ring Kichard, yes...but surely that's not an anagram, that's a spoonerism.

MAN: If you're going to split hairs I'm going to piss off.

chez rat

Hors D'Oeuvres

Soup of the Day (nearly always rat)

Melon Venezia (succulent honeydew melon, soaked in Kirsch, with a dead rat on top)

Ratatouille

Escargot (really rat)

Entrées

Rat au Vin (fresh rat killed with a chopper held up against the glinting sunlight and brought down with a terrific wham! on the tiny vertebrate in wine)

Rat au Poivre (the same only more violent)

Rat à Tué (unlimited rats killed at your table by the method of your own choice)

Rat Muré (large black rats hurled at a wall by the chef)

Dessert

Rats (various)

Coffee and rats 40p extra

chez rat

BANTER

"Somewhere in England, 1944". The squadron leader enters an RAF officers' mess and takes off his helmet.

BOVRIL: Morning, Squadron Leader.

SQUADRON LEADER: What-ho, Squiffy.

BOVRIL: How was it?

SQUADRON LEADER: Top hole. Bally Jerry pranged his kite right in the how's your father. Hairy blighter, dicky-birdied, feathered back on his Sammy, took a waspy, flipped over his Betty Harper's and caught his can in the Bertie.

BOVRIL: Er, I'm afraid I don't quite follow you, Squadron Leader.

SQUADRON LEADER: It's perfectly ordinary banter, Squiffy. Bally Jerry...pranged his kite, right in the how's yer father...hairy blighter, dicky-birdied, feathered back on his Sammy, took a waspy, flipped over on his Betty Harper's and caught his can in the Bertie.

BOVRIL: No, I'm just not understanding banter at all well today. Give us it slower.

SQUADRON LEADER: Banter's not the *same* if you say it slower, Squiffy.

BOVRIL: Hold on, then. *(shouts)* Wingco!

WINGCO: Yes!

BOVRIL: Bend an ear to the Squadron Leader's banter for a sec, would you?

WINGCO: Can do.

BOVRIL: Jolly good.

WINGCO: Fire away.

SQUADRON LEADE: *(draws a deep breath and looks slightly uncertain, then starts even more deliberately than before)*: Bally Jerry...pranged his kite...right in the how's yer father...hairy blighter...dicky-birdied...feathered back on his Sammy...took a waspy...flipped over

his Betty Harper's... and caught his can in the Bertie...

WINGCO: ...No, don't understand that banter at all.

SQUADRON LEADER: Something up with my banter, chaps?

A siren goes. The door bursts open and an out-of-breath young pilot rushes in in his flying gear.

PILOT: Bunch of monkeys on the ceiling, sir! Grab your egg and fours and let's get the bacon delivered.

General incomprehension. They look at each other.

WINGCO: Do you understand that?

SQUADRON LEADER: No, didn't get a word of it.

WINGCO: Sorry old man, we don't understand your banter.

PILOT: You know...bally ten-penny ones dropping in the custard...*(searching for the words)* um...Charlie Choppers chucking a handful...
WINGCO: No, no...sorry.
BOVRIL: Say it a bit slower, old chap.
PILOT: Slower banter, sir?
WINGCO: Ra-ther!
PILOT: Um...sausage squad up the blue end!
SQUADRON LEADER: No, still don't get it.
PILOT: Um...cabbage crates coming over the briny?
SQUADRON LEADER: No.
OTHERS: No, no...
VOICE OVER: But by then it was too late. The first cabbage crates hit London on July 7th. That was just the beginning...

THE OXFOD SIMPLIFIED
DICTIONARY

A

A a

Aard-vark a very difficult word which you don't need to know.

Abacinate another word which is totally useless and you won't ever use so don't go fretting over it or looking it up in another dictionary because honestly its pointless

Aback aback

Abacus a very similar word to "Aback".

Abalone *see* "Aard-vark"

Abandon to abandon

Abbey an abbey

Abbot an abbot

Abbreviate to abbreviate

Abdicate to abdicate

Abdication ditto near enough

Abditory also similar

Abdomen same again except for five letters

Abduct almost the same

Aberration an almost totally different word - ignore it

Abettor abdomen

Abeyance *see* "Aard-vark"

Knickers ladies' underpants

Abhorrent I wouldn't worry about what this word means

Abide abdicate

Abigail lady's maid

Ability ability

Abject abdicate

Abjure abject (only three letters' difference and they try to pass it off as a different word! Just shows those mealy-mouthed egg-heads in the universities haven't got anything better to do than split hairs over tiny little details that don't make a fart of difference to people's lives. Abject/abjure what's the difference? Who cares anyway?)

Ablative This kind of thing makes me sick! Does it matter a tinker's cuss what different endings they used to have in a language nobody speaks any more.

Ablaze ablaze

Able able

Abnegate to abjure! (It really is! Look it up in the O.E.D. if you don't believe me!)

Abnormal abnormal

Aboard aboard

Abode abode

Abolish abolish (this is what dictionaries ought to be like)

Abominable abominable

Abound abound

About about

Above above

Abracadabra abracadabra

Hey presto! hey presto!

Shazam! shazam!

Oogie-woogie it's a boogie

Abreast *not* "a breast"

Abroad practically the same as "Aboard" - in fact it's just got one tiny weeny little letter in a different place and they try to pass it off as a different word! Therefore, very definitely, *see* "Aboard".

Abrupt abrupt

Abscess a collection of pus or purulent matter formed by a morbid process in a cavity of the body. Great! It's words like that that make a dictionary really worthwhile.

Absolute absolute

Absolution absolute

Absolutist absolute

Absolutory absolute

Absolve absolute

Absonant absolute

Absorb absolute

Abstract abstract

Abuse abuse

Abyss abyss

Acadialte oh piss off.

B

Buttock buttock

Bum bum

Tit tit

This is the end of the "Oxfod Simplified Dictionary". Words beginning with the letter C onwards are seldom used, and are hardly worth including in a genuine simplified dictionary. N.B. We do not refund money to clever-dicks who want to look up other words. So there. Ed.

THE MINISTER FOR
NOT LISTENING TO PEOPLE

The Minister for not listening to people toured Batley today to investigate allegations of victimization in home-loan improvement grants, made last week by the Shadow Minister for judging people at first sight to be marginally worse than they actually are. At the Home Office, the Minister for inserting himself in between chairs and walls in men's clubs, was at his desk after a short illness. He spent the morning dealing with the Irish situation and later in the day had long discussions with the Minister for running upstairs two at a time, flinging the door open and saying "Ha, ha! Caught you, Mildred". In the Commons there was another day of heated debate on the third reading of the Trade Practices Bill. Mr Roland Penrose, the Under-Secretary for making deep growling noises grrr, launched a bitter personal attack on the ex-Minister for delving deep into a black satin bag and producing a tube of Euthymol toothpaste. Later in the debate the Junior Minister for being frightened by any kind of farm machinery, challenged the Under-Secretary of State for hiding from Terence Rattigan to produce the current year's trading figures, as supplied by the Department of stealing packets of bandages from the self-service counter at Timothy Whites and selling them again at a considerable profit. Parliament rose at 11.30, and, crawling along a dark passageway into the old rectory broke down the door to the serving hatch, painted the spare room and next weekend I think they'll be able to make a start on the boy's bedroom, while Amy and Roger, up in London for a few days, go to see the mysterious Mr Grenville.

THE COURT MARTIAL OF SAPPER WALTERS

A courtroom in the 1940s. A court martial is in progress. An elderly general presides, with two others on either side of him. There is a defence counsel, a prosecutor, a clerk of court, and two men guarding the prisoner.

PRESIDING GENERAL: Sapper Walters, you stand before this court accused of carrying on the war by other than warlike means – to wit, that you did on April 16th, 1942, dressed up as a bag of dainties, flick wet towels at the enemy during an important offensive...

WALTERS: Well, sir...

PRESIDING GENERAL: Shut up! Colonel Fawcett for the prosecution...

FAWCETT: Sir, we all know...

PRESIDING GENERAL: Shut up!

FAWCETT: I'm sorry?

PRESIDING GENERAL: Carry on.

FAWCETT: Sir, we all know the facts of the case; that Sapper Walters, being in possession of expensive military equipment, to wit one Lee Enfield .303 Rifle and 72 rounds of ammunition, valued at a hundred and forty pounds three shillings and sixpence, chose instead to use wet towels to take an enemy company post in the area of Basingstoke...

PRESIDING GENERAL: Basingstoke? Basingstoke in Hampshire?

FAWCETT: No, no, no, sir, no.

PRESIDING GENERAL: I see, carry on.

FAWCETT: The result of his action was that

the enemy...

PRESIDING GENERAL: Basingstoke *where?*

FAWCETT: Basingstoke, Westphalia, sir.

PRESIDING GENERAL: Oh I *see*. Carry on.

FAWCETT: The result of Sapper Walter's action was that the enemy received wet patches upon their trousers and in some cases small red strawberry marks upon their thighs...

PRESIDING GENERAL: I didn't know there *was* a Basingstoke in Westphalia.

FAWCETT *(slightly irritated)*: It's on the map, sir.

PRESIDING GENERAL: What map?

FAWCETT *(more irritably)*: The map of Westphalia as used by the army, sir.

PRESIDING GENERAL: Well, I've certainly never heard of Basingstoke in Westphalia.

FAWCETT *(patiently)*: It's a municipal borough, sir, twenty-seven miles north north east of Southampton. Its chief manufactures...

PRESIDING GENERAL: What...Southampton in Westphalia?

FAWCETT: Yes sir...bricks...clothing. Nearby are the remains of Basing House, burned down by Cromwell's cavalry in 1645...

PRESIDING GENERAL: Who compiled this map?

FAWCETT: Cole Porter, sir.

PRESIDING GENERAL *(incredulously)*: Cole Porter...who wrote *Kiss Me Kate?*

FAWCETT: No, alas not, sir...this was Cole Porter who wrote "Anything Goes". Sir, I shall seek to prove that the man before this court...

PRESIDING GENERAL: That's the same one!

(he sings) "In olden days a glimpse
of stocking..."

FAWCETT: I *beg* your pardon, sir?

PRESIDING GENERAL *(singing)*: "In olden days a glimpse of stocking, was looked on as something shocking, now heaven knows, anything goes..."

FAWCETT: No, this one's different, sir.

PRESIDING GENERAL: How does it go?

FAWCETT: What, sir?

PRESIDING GENERAL: How does *your* "Anything Goes" go?

WALTERS: Can I go home now?

PRESIDING GENERAL: Shut up! *(to Fawcett)* Come on!

FAWCETT: Sir, really, this is rather...

PRESIDING GENERAL: Come on, how does your "Anything Goes" go?

FAWCETT *(clearing his throat and going into an extraordinary tuneless and very loud song)*

> Anything goes in.
> Anything goes out!
> Fish, bananas, old pyjamas,
> Mutton! Beef! and Trout!
> Anything goes in...

PRESIDING GENERAL: No, that's not it...carry on.

FAWCETT: With respect sir, I shall seek to prove that the man before you in the dock, being in possession of the following: one pair of army boots, value three pounds seven and six, one pair of serge trousers, value two pounds three and six, one pair of gaiters value sixty-eight pounds ten shillings, one...

PRESIDING GENERAL: Sixty-eight pounds ten shillings for a pair of *gaiters*?

FAWCETT *(dismissively)*: They were special gaiters, sir.

PRESIDING GENERAL: *Special* gaiters?

FAWCETT: Yes sir, they were made in France. One beret costing four-teen shillings, one pair of...

PRESIDING GENERAL: What was so special about them?

FAWCETT: Oh...*(as if he can hardly be bothered to reply)* they were made of a special fabric, sir. The buckles were made of empire silver instead of brass. The total value of the uniform was there...

PRESIDING GENERAL: Why was the accused wearing special gaiters?

FAWCETT *(irritably)*: They were a presentation pair, from the regiment. The total value of the uniform...

PRESIDING GENERAL: Why did they present him with a special pair of gaiters?

FAWCETT: Sir, it seems to me totally irrelevant to the case whether the gaiters were presented to him or not, sir.

PRESIDING GENERAL: I think the court will be able to judge that for them-selves. I want to know why the regiment presented the accused with a special pair of gaiters.

FAWCETT *(stifling his impatience)*: He...used to do things for them. The total value...

PRESIDING GENERAL: What things?

FAWCETT *(exasperated)*: He...used to oblige them, sir. The total value...

PRESIDING GENERAL: *Oblige* them?

FAWCETT: Yes sir. The total value of the uniform...

PRESIDING GENERAL: How did he *oblige* them?

FAWCETT *(more and more irritated)*: He...um...he used to make them happy in little ways, sir. The total value of the uniform could there-fore not have been less than...

PRESIDING GENERAL: Did he touch them at all?

FAWCETT: Sir! I submit that this is totally irrelevant.

PRESIDING GENERAL: I want to know how he made them happy.

FAWCETT *(losing his temper)*: He used to ram things up their...

PRESIDING GENERAL *(quickly)*: All right! All right! No need to spell it out! What er...what has the accused got to say?

WALTERS *(taken off guard)*: What, me?

PRESIDING GENERAL: Yes. What have you got to say?

WALTERS: What can I say? I mean, how can I encapsulate in mere words my scorn for any military solution? The futility of modern warfare? And the hypocrisy by which contemporary government applies one standard to violence within the community and another to violence perpetrated by one community upon another?

DEFENCE COUNSEL: I'm sorry, but my client has become pretentious. I will say in his defence that he has suffered...

FAWCETT: Sir! We haven't finished the prosecution!

PRESIDING COUNSEL: Shut up! I'm in charge of this court. *(to the court)* Stand up! *(everyone stands up)* Sit down! *(everyone sits down)* Go moo! *(everyone goes moo; the presiding general turns to Fawcett)* See? Right, now, on with the pixie hats! *(everyone puts on pixie hats with large pointed ears)* And order in the skating vicar. *(a skating vicar enters and everyone bursts into song)*

EVERYONE: Anything goes in.
Anything goes out!
Fish, bananas, old pyjamas,
Mutton! Beef! and Trout!
Anything goes in.
Anything goes out
Fish, bananas, old pyjamas,
Mutton! Beef! and Trout!

MRS O: Morning Mrs Trepidatious.

WHAT THE ST★RS REALLY SAY

MRS TREPIDATIOUS: Oh, I don't know what's good about it, my right arm's hanging off something awful.

MRS O: Oh, you want to have that seen to.

MRS TREPIDATIOUS: What, by that Dr Morrison? He's killed more patients than I've had severe boils.

MRS O: What do the stars say?

MRS TREPIDATIOUS: Well, Petula Clark says burst them early, but David Frost...

MRS O: No, the stars in the paper, you cloth-eared heap of anteater's catarrh, the zodiacal signs, the horoscopic fates, the astrological portents, the omens, the genethliac prognostications, the mantological harbingers, the vaticinal utterances, the fratridical premonitory uttering of the mantological omens - what do the bleeding stars in the paper predict, forecast, prophesy, foretell, prognosticate...

A big sheet is lowered with the words on

VOICE OVER: And this is where you at home can join in.

MRS O: ...forebode, bode, augur, spell, foretoken, presage, portend, foreshow, foreshadow, forerun, herald, point to, betoken, indicate!

MRS TREPIDATIOUS: I don't know.

The sheet is raised again

MRS O: What are you?

MRS TREPIDATIOUS: I'm Nesbitt.

MRS O: There's not a zodiacal sign called Nesbitt.

MRS TREPIDATIOUS: All right, Derry and Toms.

MRS O *(surveying the paper)*: Aquarius, Scorpio, Virgo, Derry and Toms. April 29th to March 22nd. Even dates only.

MRS TREPIDATIOUS: Well what does it presage?

MRS O: You have green, scaly skin, and a soft yellow underbelly with a series of fin-like ridges running down your spine and tail. Although lizardlike in shape, you can grow anything up to thirty feet in length with huge teeth that can bite off great rocks and trees. You inhabit arid sub-tropical zones and wear spectacles.

MRS TREPIDATIOUS: It's very good about the spectacles.

MRS O: It's amazing.

MRS TREPIDATIOUS: Mm...what's yours, Irene?

MRS O: Basil.

MRS TREPIDATIOUS: I'm sorry, what's yours, Basil?

MRS O: No. That's my star sign, Basil...

MRS TREPIDATIOUS: There isn't a...

MRS O: Yes there is...Aquarius, Sagittarius, Derry and Toms, Basil. June 21st to June 22nd.

MRS TREPIDATIOUS: Well, what does it say?

MRS O: You have green, scaly skin and a series of yellow underbellies running down your spine and tail...

MRS TREPIDATIOUS: That's exactly the same!

MRS O. Try number one...what's Aquarius?

MRS TREPIDATIOUS: It's a zodiacal sign.

MRS O: I know that, what does it say in the paper Mrs Flan-and-pickle?

MRS TREPIDATIOUS: All right...Oh! It says, "a wonderful day ahead". You will be surrounded by family and friends. Roger Moore will drop in for lunch, bringing Tony Curtis with him. In the afternoon a substantial cash sum will come your way. In the evening Petula Clark will visit your home accompanied by the Mike Sammes singers. She will sing for you in your own living room. Before you go to bed, Peter Wyngarde will come and declare his undying love for you.

MRS O: Urghh! What's Scorpio?

MRS TREPIDATIOUS: Oh, that's very good. "You will have lunch with a school-friend of Duane Eddy's, who will insist on whistling some of Duane's greatest instrumental hits. In the afternoon you will die, you will be buried..."

THE GALAXY
SONG

That's orbiting at nineteen miles a second, so it's reckoned,
A sun that is the source of all our power.
The sun and you and me and all the stars that we can see,
Are moving at a million miles a day
In an outer spiral arm, at forty thousand miles an hour,
Of the galaxy we call the Milky Way.

Our galaxy itself contains a hundred billion stars
It's a hundred thousand light years side to side.
It bulges in the middle sixteen thousand light years thick
But out by us its just three thousand light years wide.
We're thirty thousand light years from galactic central point,
We go round every two hundred million years
And our galaxy is only one of millions of billions
In this amazing and expanding Universe.

The Universe itself keeps expanding and expanding
In all of the directions it can whizz
As fast as it can go, at the speed of light you know,
Twelve million miles a minute, and that's the fastest speed there is.
So remember when you're feeling very small and insecure
How amazingly unlikely is your birth
And pray that there's intelligent life somewhere up in space
Because there's bugger all down here on earth.

257

BIBLIOGRAPHY

If you enjoyed this book here are a few more books that you may enjoy but probably not.

Non-Fiction

The Boys' Book of Burglary
Breaking and Entering For Beginners
Do's and Don'ts For the First-Time House- Breaker
Violent Intrusion Made Easy
A Primer of Larceny With Menaces
Why Have Locks?
The Evils of Home Security Systems
Why You Should Never Bolt Your Doors
The Practical Home-Builder's Manual Number Five: Leaving Valuables About For All to See When They Look In Your Windows
Burglars Have to Live Too
Neighbourhood Watch (A Tale of Treachery and Horror)
My Burglar, My Friend
Why It Makes Sense To Spryzgee
The A to Z of B To Y
The Royal Britannia Encyclopaedia of Very Small Holes Made In Metal Surfaces By Certain Kinds of Filament Under Certain Conditions (not recommended)
The Bumper Book of Very Easy Facts Made Very Simple For People With Very Small Brains
The Bumper Book of Very Easy Facts Made Very Simple For People With Very Small Brains But With Pictures of Girls With Large Breasts (A *Sun* Special)
Raspberryade - The Extraordinary Exposé
Raspberryade - An Apology
Raspberryade - The True Story Behind the Revelations Scandal

Raspberryade - At Last! The True Facts!
Raspberryade - What Was it All About?
The Wonderful World of Chicken Sexing
How To Turn Unwanted Clothing Into Pastrami Sandwiches
The Art of Cooking With Motor Oil
Cooking With Poisonous Mushrooms (Ideal for those who hate cooking for
    friends)
Cooking Delia Smith
Cooking With Delia Smith - (Contains an Apology for the previous edition)
Eating Well - Drinking Badly - A Guide To Thoroughly Enjoying Yourself
Eating Well - Drinking Badly - Throwing-up Often (sequel)
The Air-Hostesses' Guide To Passengers Who Are Looking For A One -Night Stand
The Air-Hostesses' Guide To Male Passengers Who Are Looking For A
    One-Night Stand With No Strings And No Exchange of Addresses
The Air-Hostesses' Guide To Wealthy Male Passengers Who Are Looking
    For A One-Night Stand But May Be Willing To Turn It Into A Longer Term
    Relationship Though Without Committing To Any Binding Financial
    Arrangement After Only One Night - Understandably
The Air- Hostesses' Guide To Passengers Who Are Looking For A One-
    Night Stand On Condition That They Can Also Speak To The Pilot First
The Air- Hostesses' Guide To Passengers Who Are Looking For A One-Night
    Stand Without Necessarily Being Interested in Sex But Just Good Company
    And A Few Laughs And Maybe Some Pickles And A Banana Before Pissing
    Off To Their Own Hotel Room
The Air-Hostesses' Guide To Hot-Water Bottles and Comfortable Bedsocks
The Wonderful World Of Wheel-Balancing - by Ken U.R. Dull

Fiction
The Wonderful War On Serbia - How It Saved Lives And Established A
    Lasting Peace In The Balkans

259

SELECTED
BY
JOHN
CLEESE

WITH A PREFACE BY MICHAEL PALIN

It is indeed an honour to be able to pen a few words by way of introduction to John's selection of Python literary memorabilia. Well, quite an honour. Actually, it's a bit of a bloody nuisance as I'd hoped to have the afternoon off for a massage. Fortunately I have a Heartfelt Tributes programme on my computer. All I have to do, in theory, is tap in the recipient's name – John Cleese, The Queen Mother, Saddam Hussein – and Hey presto! Microsoft does the business, and I'm on the table beneath Suki's healing, if not yet fully licensed hands, within the hour. So, here goes, install programme and press 'Enter'.

A Heartfelt Tribute to John Cleese

John Cleese is one of those rare people, like Bill Gates, who has been blessed with enormous natural talent and, more importantly, the ability to harness it for the good of mankind. In the same way that Bill Gates was able to realise his vision of, quite literally creating a new world order through his own single-minded brilliance in the creation of computer technology, so John Cleese has done whatever he has done so well.

Bill Gates, unlike the Queen Mother, is not a man who flaunts his own personal power. He is essentially a modest man. A man whose only hope is that the world becomes a better place to live in, that it becomes a world where, thanks to spell-check and effective file management, little children cease to cry and animals give milk and the halt walk and the lame dance and people with no talent for anything just buy the stuff and shut up and let people like John and Bill and Saddam get on with what they do best... RUNNING THE WORLD !!!!!!!

Some kind of virus seems to have crept into the Heartfelt Tributes '97 programme, either that or I'm not using it properly, so I shall have to do the damn preface myself and put Suki off until tomorrow and hope that the groin strain doesn't get any worse. Sorry about all this. I'll be as quick as I can.

John Cleese - The Writer's writer.
A personal appreciation by Michael Palin.

John loves words, particularly 'nebulous', 'trenchant' and 'orthodontic'. Though most children's first word is 'mama', John's was 'elision'. 'Mama' was third, after 'hydraulics'.

Even his birthplace, Weston-Super-Mare, had two words more than most people's birthplaces. He has written many words for Monty Python, some of which like 'parrot', 'cheese' and 'breasts' have gone down in history.

Rumours abound about this tower of talent, ranging from the fantastic - he once tunnelled under the Grand National course at Aintree and stuck a spoon up through the turf five days after the race had passed - through the frankly unlikely - he can take out his intestines and put them back again without surgery, to the intriguing - he is related on his mother's side to Prester John. Whatever the truth about this deeply private man one thing is certain, he was born with a silver tongue in his mouth.

John's favourite authors are eighteen and female.

M.P. June 1999

Eric the half a bee

Half a bee, philosophically,
Must, ipso facto, half not be.
But half the bee has got to be,
Vis-à-vis its entity. D'you see?
But can a bee be said to be,
Or not to be, an entire bee,
When half the bee is not a bee,
Due to some ancient injury?

La di di, one two three,
Eric the half a bee.
A b c d e f g,
Eric the half a bee.

Is this wretched demi-bee,
Half asleep upon my knee,
Some freak from a menagerie?
No! It's Eric the half a bee.

Fiddle di dum, fiddle di dee,
Eric the half a bee.
Ho ho ho,
Tee hee hee,
Eric the half a bee.

I love this hive employ-ee-ee,
Bisected accidentally,
One summer afternoon by me,
I love him carnally.
Semi-carnally.
The end.

Cyril Connolly?

No, semi-carnally!

Oh.

ANNE ELK'S
THEORY

PRESENTER: I have with me tonight an elk. Oh! *Anne* Elk.

MISS ELK: Miss Anne Elk

PRESENTER: Now I understand you have a new theory about the brontosaurus, Miss Elk.

MISS ELK: Can I just say here Chris, for one moment, that I have a new theory about the brontosaurus?

PRESENTER: Exactly ... What is it?

MISS ELK: Where?

PRESENTER: No, no, your new theory.

MISS ELK: Oh! What is my theory?

PRESENTER: Yes.

MISS ELK: Oh what is my theory, that it is. Well Chris, you may well ask me what is my theory.

PRESENTER: ... Yes, I *am* asking you.

MISS ELK: Thank you, Chris. Well Chris, what is it, that it is - this theory of mine? Well, this is what it is - my theory that I have, that is to say, which is mine ... is mine.

PRESENTER: ... Yes, I *know* it's yours, but what is it?

MISS ELK: Where? Oh, what is my theory? This is it. *(She clears her throat at some length)* My theory, that belongs to me, is as follows. *(She clears her throat at greater length)* This is how it goes. The next thing that I am going to say, is my theory. Ready?

PRESENTER: Yes!

MISS ELK: My theory by A. Elk. Brackets, Miss, brackets. This theory goes as follows, and begins now. All brontosauruses are thin at one end, much much thicker in the middle and then thin again at the far end. That is my theory, which is mine, and belongs to me and I own it, and what it is too.

thinner · *thicker* · *thinner*

PRESENTER: ... That's it, is it?

MISS ELK: Spot on, Chris.

PRESENTER: Well, this theory of yours appears to have ... er ... hit the nail on the head.

MISS ELK: *And* it's mine.

PRESENTER: Yes, well thank you very much for coming along to the studio.

MISS ELK: My pleasure, Chris.

The Official Medallic Commemoration of the History of Mankind

Hallmarked First Edition Proof Sets in solid Welsh Silver* are available ONLY by advance covenanted subscription or, of course, cash. To preserve value, the number of sets minted must be strictly limited to the number we can actually sell. No more will be minted after this number is reached, in order to guarantee rarity.

This Magnificent Set of Shiny Bright Objects will be of particular interest, not only to everyone, but especially to Collectors of Objets d'Art and Jackdaws.

ABSOLUTELY FREE!

All Hallmarked First Edition Proof Sets are clearly marked 'Hallmarked First Edition Proof Set' to distinguish them from Non-Hallmarked First Edition Proof Sets, and Hallmarked Second (or Third) Edition Proof Sets, and Hallmarked First Edition Non-Proof Sets, none of which exists. However the words 'Hallmarked First Edition' and 'Proof' have associations with objects of value and so are clearly marked on these medallions.

*A very attractive and valuable Zinc / Bakelite alloy

Jack Hobbs stabbed in his bath by Charlotte Rampling

Napoleon forging luncheon vouchers

Marie Curie eludes Nero's troops by hiding in a lift

Leonardo da Vinci nearly inventing Canasta

George Washington shortly before intercourse with Mary Baker Eddy

Oliver Cromwell in Stand by Your Bedouin *with Brian Rix*

Peter the Great carving his initials on a passing vicar

Mrs René Descartes sleeping

The vital, dramatic and very fascinating history of Man himself, which will be of particular interest to all human beings, is now to be made official, by the issue of these fine medallions, with nice pictures on them, and not too many words.

RAYMOND
LUXURY YACHT

INTERVIEWER: Good evening. I have with me in the studio tonight one of Britain's leading skin specialists – Raymond Luxury Yacht.

RAYMOND: That's not my name.

INTERVIEWER: I'm sorry.

RAYMOND: It's spelt Raymond Luxury Yacht, but it's pronounced 'Throatwobbler Mangrove'.

INTERVIEWER: ...You're a very silly man and I'm not going to interview you.

RAYMOND: Ah, anti-Semitism!

INTERVIEWER: ...Not at all. That's not even a proper nose. It's polystyrene.

He takes Raymond's nose off.

RAYMOND: Give me my nose back.

INTERVIEWER: You can collect it at reception. Now go away.

RAYMOND: I want to be on the television.

INTERVIEWER: Well you can't.

African Notebook

by Col. B. B. Wakenham-Palsh M.C., O.B.E.

Chapter 19
A Lucky Escape

The next day I decided to take my usual pre-breakfast 'stroll', as I used to call it, into the *majambi,* or jungle, to see if I could catch sight of the very rare 'Chukawati Bati' or Bird of Purgatory, which 'Trusty' as we all called our faithful native *ghabi* or guide had reported seeing the previous *latbani* (evening) while we were looking for Harry's leg.

I had only been 'strolling' along the *majambi* (jungle) *ortobam* (path) for a few minutes when I became aware of a large and rather fierce *fritbangowonkabwaki,* or lion, which was standing partially hidden in the *pteee,* or clearing. I had strayed so close to him, absorbed as I was in my ornithological *questi* (quest) that when the splendid old thing opened its massive *goti* (jaws) to roar, revealing as fine a *womba,* or set, of teeth as I have seen in an adult male, I could, without so much as leaning forward, have taken his magnificent uvula in my left hand. Taking advantage of my good luck, I did so, tweaking it hard, an old English colonial officer's *granwi,* or trick. This bemused the lion and so I was able to get in a couple of good straight lefts, keeping my guard up well, to his upper palate and follow them with a cracking good right cross, moving my weight into the punch (as old 'Buffy' Spalding had taught me so many years ago, prior to the needle

11

match against Uppington when 'Spindly' Crabber got up off the floor six times so pluckily only just to fail to win the draw which would have halved the *batwel* or match), right into my opponent's mane. Then dancing back a couple of paces, I weaved about causing *fritbangowonkabwaki* to miss wildly with his crude haymakers while I notched up a few useful points with my left *swati,* or hand, and I soon found that by this simple strategy of keeping him from getting in close, where his mighty jaws could have done a lot of *nagasaki,* or damage, I could pick him off pretty much at leisure. In fact it was only after some *twenti (*twenty) minutes that I happened to glance around the clearing to discover that our contest was now being watched by a circle of some fifteen odd of *fritbangowonkabwaki's* chums, some of whom were already beginning to edge forward, manes bristling and teeth akimbo, towards our good selves.

It was the work of a moment to divine from their magnificent expressions that they were taking a decidedly partisan attitude to our match, and that they would have few qualms about joining in on my opponent's side if necessary; and so, judging that, if they did, they would eventually subdue me by sheer weight of numbers, I took the better part of valour, and feinting away from another of *fritbangowonkabwaki's* wild rushes, I got in a parting short jab to the

base of his tail (not a blow I was proud of, although it put him down for several minutes, but which I felt was excused by the exigencies of the situation, due, after all, to the unsporting behaviour of his colleagues in the first place) before springing upwards towards a lowly hanging branch of an enormous *bwinda tree* (a species related distantly to our own *Elm* (elm), but easily distinguishable by its broad unevenly veined leaf, with its characteristic cheetah's paw shape, and the peculiar purple-ochre colour of the outer leaves of its *gimbi*, or buds), some fifteen feet  above my head. I had leapt not a moment too soon, for, although I had gained a firm grasp upon the handy branch, two of *fritbangowonkabwaki's* pals, leaping with me, had each seized one of my trusty boots in their jaws whilst a third had succeeded in firmly embedding his *jangi* (teeth) in the seat of my pants, albeit not in my *sit-upon* itself, but in the surrounding material thereof. What a strange sight I must have made, hanging unshaven from the branch with three enormous lions attached to me! It was not, indeed, without difficulty that I pulled myself up until I could take the branch in my mouth, thus freeing my hands for the more important work of detaching the determined trio, whose bites, however, proved to be so *woki,* or vice-like, that I eventually decided, not without regret, that it was only by actually abandoning the relevant apparel that I could free myself of their attentions.

Unlacing a jungle boot while hanging by one's teeth from a tree with three angry lions attached is not as easy as it might seem, especially when the lions concerned are being urged on to even greater efforts by the highly vocal support of their companions beneath, but eventually it was done, and right boot and lion plummeted back into the clearing, followed rapidly by their opposite numbers. With the vastly reduced load the shorts were a formality and in a trice I was seated comfortably on the branch looking down at the enraged pride beneath, who by now, incidentally, must have numbered well over a hundred. However, by now I was feeling distinctly peckish , and so doffing my *sola topi* rather humorously in their direction I turned for home and breakfast.

As I made my way back to camp through the trees some *jambotwanibokotwikatwanafryingpanibwanabotomafekazami* (five) minutes later, with the lions still pursuing me below, I saw that I had reached the Wananga River. To my delight, I spotted a solitary creeper suspended from a tree just upstream, across the cascading torrent, to the forest the other side. Ideal! Soon I was well on my way towards the far bank, admiring the magnificent view of the raging Wananga directly beneath. However, I was still not half-way across when I began to realise that my 'creeper' was not all it might be, and looking towards the far end of it I was astonished to see, staring back at me from a wak-wak tree, the unmistakable square head, yellow-green criss-cross markings and fearful fangs of an anaconda! I will admit I was astounded! An anaconda in Africa! And what is more, one that clearly took exception to being demoted to viaduct. With one mighty flick of its rippling body, I was sent spinning high, high up into the air, where I had to dodge a passing eagle, before being able to plunge downwards into the waiting *ouse* (river).

I had already surmised that my new surroundings would pose a different problem, for the Wananga is notorious for both the quantity of its hippopotamus and crocodile, and also for the degree of rancour with which these two species regard the human race, and sure enough, on surfacing, I saw the huge shapes of the former

14

setting off towards me from their station upstream, while several thousand of the latter bore down on me from the other direction; so, making the best of a bad job, I swam straight at the nearest crocodile, waited until he opened his enormous jaws and then quick as a flash spurted forward and, snatching a full lungful of air, hurled myself into his mouth, pulling the jaws shut after me, and scrambled down his throat, while he was still surprised, to the relative safety of his stomach, where I stayed, holding my breath, until I guessed the coast was clear. Then gambling all on a quick getaway, I worked my way back up his thorax and started insistently tickling the back of his throat. I did not have long to wait, for the jaws opened suddenly and I was hurled out into the light of day by the force of the mightiest cough I have ever experienced at such close quarters, right onto the bank of the river, believe it or not about ten yards from the point where the rest of the fellows were just tucking into their devilled kidneys. I must say they were pretty amused to see me appearing from a nearby crocodile without my shorts, but I took their jesting in good part and had soon rejoined them to salvage what I could from the pan of kidneys.

It may seem that I have rather padded out a commonplace enough tale, but the real reason that I have recounted my adventure in perhaps rather unnecessary detail is that *exactly* the same thing happened to my wife the very next day.

CONSULTING
JEAN-PAUL SARTRE

MRS CONCLUSION: Hello, Mrs Premise.

MRS PREMISE: Hello, Mrs Conclusion.

MRS CONCLUSION: Busy day?

MRS PREMISE: Busy! I've just spent four hours burying the cat.

MRS CONCLUSION: *Four* hours to bury a cat?

MRS PREMISE: Yes! It wouldn't keep still, wriggling about, howling its head off.

MRS CONCLUSION: Oh – it wasn't dead then?

MRS PREMISE: Well, no, no, but it's not at all a well cat, so as we were going away for a fortnight's holiday, I thought I'd better bury it, just to be on the safe side.

MRS CONCLUSION: Quite right. You don't want to come back from Sorrento to a dead cat. That's bathos that is. Yes, kill it now, that's what I say. We're going to have our budgie put down.

MRS PREMISE: Is it very old?

MRS CONCLUSION: No, we just don't like it. We're going to take it to the vet tomorrow.

MRS PREMISE: Tell me, how do they put budgies down then?

MRS CONCLUSION: Well it's funny you should ask that, but I've just been reading a great big book about how to put your budgie down, and apparently you can either hit them with the book, or, you can shoot them just there, just above the beak.

MRS PREMISE: Well well well. 'Course, Mrs Essence flushed hers down the loo.

MRS CONCLUSION: Ooh! No! You shouldn't do that – it's dangerous. They breed in the sewers, and eventually you get evil-smelling flocks of huge soiled budgies flying out of people's lavatories infringing their personal freedom.

MRS PREMISE: It's a funny thing freedom. I mean how can any of us be really free when we still have personal possessions?

MRS CONCLUSION: You can't. I mean, how can I go off and join Frelimo when I've got nine more instalments to pay on the fridge?

MRS PREMISE: Well this is the whole crux of Jean-Paul Sartre's *Roads to Freedom*.

MRS CONCLUSION: No, it bloody isn't. The nub of that is, his characters stand for all of us in their desire to avoid action. Mind you, the man at the off-licence says it's an everyday story of French country folk.

MRS PREMISE: What does he know? Sixty new pence for a bottle of Maltese Claret! Well I personally think Jean-Paul's masterwork is an allegory of man's search for commitment.

MRS CONCLUSION: No it isn't.

MRS PREMISE: All right. We can soon settle this. We'll ask him.

MRS CONCLUSION: ... Do you know him?

MRS PREMISE: Yes, we met on holiday last year.

MRS CONCLUSION: In Ibiza!?

MRS PREMISE: Off we go.

MRS PREMISE: Oh look, Paris!

Mrs Conclusion and Mrs Premise walk up to the front door of an apartment block. On the front door is a list of the inhabitants of the block.

4. JEAN GENET & FRIEND

8. Mr René Descartes (junior)

FLAT 3 JACQUES COUSTEAU

7. Jean-Paul Sartre et Betty-Muriel Sartre

2 Yves Montand

flat 6 Indira Gandhi

Flat 1 Duke & Duchess of Windsor

FLAT 5. MARCEL MARCEAU WALKING AGAINST THE WIND LIMITED

MRS SARTRE: Hello, love!

MRS PREMISE: Hello! Oh this is Mrs Conclusion from No.46.

MRS SARTRE: Nice to meet you, dear.

MRS CONCLUSION: Bonjour.

MRS PREMISE: How's the old man, then?

MRS SARTRE: Oh, don't ask. He's in one of his bleeding moods. 'The bourgeoisie *this*, the bourgeoisie *that*'...

MRS PREMISE: Can we have a word with him?

MRS SARTRE: Yes.

MRS CONCLUSION: Thank you.

Mrs Premise and Mrs Conclusion go and knock on the door of Jean-Paul's room.

MRS PREMISE: Coo-ee! Jean-Paul?

JEAN-PAUL'S VOICE: Oui?

MRS PREMISE: Jean-Paul. Your famous trilogy *Les Chemins de la Liberté*, is it an allegory of man's search for commitment?

JEAN-PAUL'S VOICE: Oui.

MRS PREMISE: I told you so!

MRS CONCLUSION: Oh *sugar*!

WE'RE ALL INDIVIDUALS

BRIAN wakes, stretches and goes to open his bedroom shutters.

CROWD: HOSANNA!!

BRIAN: ...Good morning.

CROWD: A blessing! A blessing!

BRIAN: No, please. Please!! Please listen...

The crowd quietens.

BRIAN: I've got one or two things to say.

CROWD: Tell us. Tell us *both* of them!!

BRIAN: Look ... you've got it all wrong. You don't need to follow me. You don't need to follow anybody. You've got to think for yourselves — you're all individuals.

CROWD: Yes, we're all individuals.

BRIAN: You are all *different*.

CROWD: Yes, we are all different.

MAN: I'm not.

CROWD: ssshhh!

BRIAN: ...well, that's it. You've all got to work it out for yourselves...

CROWD: Yes, yes!! We've got to work it out for *ourselves*...

BRIAN: Exactly.

CROWD: ....Tell us *more*!!!!

THE PYTHON PANEL

Ruth Frampton: Britain's first woman judge and a leading exponent of Women's Lib.
Vice-Pope Eric: the No. 2 man in the Vatican.
Brian Stalin: eldest brother of the USSR's late great Dictator.
Dr Edward Kraszt: American sociologist and author of All Anyone Need Know About Anyth

PYTHON: Good evening.

ALL EXCEPT KRASZT: Good evening.

KRASZT: I didn't say 'Good evening' then because I wanted a line to myself.

PYTHON: We take your point, Dr Kraszt. Vice-Pope Eric?

VICE-POPE: Not at the moment, thank you.

PYTHON: Brian?

STALIN: I'm fine thanks. How about Miss Frampton?

PYTHON: Well we are going to ask her our first question so that's not really necessary.

ALL: Fine.

PYTHON: Ruth Frampton, in 1959 you became the first woman to become a judge of Quarter Sessions in this country.

FRAMPTON: My first line is just to say 'That's right'.

PYTHON: Why do you claim to be Sir Edmund Hillary's mother?

STALIN: What? I've never said I ...

PYTHON: No, we were talking to Miss Frampton.

STALIN: Sorry, I thought you were looking at me.

KRASZT: It's a bit confusing you know.

PYTHON: Shut up please. (*Laughter*)

KRASZT: I didn't hear anyone laugh.

PYTHON: To return to our question. Why do you claim a maternal situation vis-à-vis the first conqueror of Everest?

FRAMPTON Because I *am* his mum. He is my little Edmund, bless his little pitons, and he has been a wonderful boy to me.

PYTHON: But Sir Edmund has it on record that he knows his mother well and that she and you are definitely separate persons.

FRAMPTON: Then he is being naughty because he is over-tired. All boys are

THE PYTHON
PANEL

naughty sometimes; to expect them to be perfect is quintessentially daft.

PYTHON: Dr. Kraszt?

KRASZT: This is probably correct. The recent survey of 420,000 people, carried out at Michigan University over a period of eight years by Professors Rinehart, Schwartz, Zincstein and Semite, indicates conclusively that people – not just boys, interestingly enough – are by and large not absolutely perfect. A statistically significant proportion of them, at some stage in the 70-odd-years maturation process, do something that they ought not to really. These findings constitute something of a breakthrough in this field.

PYTHON: Thank you Dr. Kraszt.

FRAMPTON: You see? So I am *definitely* his mother.

PYTHON: But were you actually present at his birth?

FRAMPTON: No. I can't claim that. At the time I was unavoidably detained at the Hague, where I had the honour to represent my country in the International Legal Championships. Edmund knows it was impossible for me to be there and has never held it against me.

STALIN: Then why is he applying for an injunction against the publication of your forthcoming book?

FRAMPTON: Because, Brian, I reveal in *My Son, The Clambering Knight* that before the final assault, he tied a large weight to Tensing so that he could get to the top first.

STALIN: Tensing's mother has confirmed this story to me. The weight, incidentally, is now in the Tensing Family Museum on K2 along with other Sherpa-connected objects.

FRAMPTON: Anyway Eddie is excrementally scared that when this gets out they will confiscate his knighthood, which would cost him a few bob in directorships. Even so, I think he has overreacted.

KRASZT: This can happen of course. People do sometimes overreact to things – that is to say, when things happen, these people – in fact, all of us – occasionally react over-wise, as it were, to these very things. To put it another way, a perfectly ordinary stimulus produces an overreaction, O. This has been shown time and time again by studies undertaken by the Californian Institute for Making Studies under Luxurious Conditions.

FRAMPTON: Exactly. Anyway, Eddie is a Kiwi poppet; it is this woman who happened to be around when he came to light who is playing dog in the manger.

PYTHON: To change the subject, how

about sex?

FRAMPTON: Sex is a fine and wonderful gift provided that it is accompanied by a feeling of love and involvement for whoever it is you happen to be banging away with at the time.

PENTHOUSE: How about pubic hair?

PYTHON: Come out from behind those curtains! Now go away and take your ludicrous catchphrases with you.

PENTHOUSE: Sorry. *(exeunt)*

PYTHON: So a feeling of love and involvement is necessary?

FRAMPTON: Or at least a reasonable pretence of it.

KRASZT: I think it's important to distinguish between premarital sex, that is sex before marriage, extra-marital sex, that is sex outside a marriage, or extra sex within; pseudo-marital sex, which is marital sex where the marriage is invalid due to an oversight in the ceremony or mistaken identity; ultra-marital sex, which is sex over and above the marital sex, quasi-marital sex where the two partners, being married, believe themselves to be making love when in fact they are not; post-marital sex which is sex after the marriage or after the divorce; and amarital sex, which is sheer simple-minded, out-of-context banging. Then there is pre-sexual marriage where the spouses are unusually timid, busy or

maladroit; extra-sexual marriage wh...

PYTHON: Vice-Pope Eric? What is the Catholic position?

VICE-POPE: Well our main worry at this stage is intra-marital sex.

PYTHON: Sex *within* the marriage.

KRASZT: I missed that.

VICE-POPE: You see, it's *within* marriage, people tend to forget, that most of this carnal knowing takes place.

PYTHON: But *that* isn't wrong from a Catholic point of view?

VICE-POPE: Well, actually ... it is. Yes. I mean we don't often come straight out with it because our problem is that ... like it or not, sex, at this moment in time, is still the best method we've got of reproducing ourselves. I mean we certainly recommend virgin births where possible, but we can't rely on them, so for purely practical reasons we've been forced to turn a blind eye to intra-marital sex *for the time being*. But only, of course, for outnumbering purposes; not for *fun*.

KRASZT: Which is why you will not allow any form of contraception.

VICE-POPE: Exactly.

FRAMPTON: But you allow the rhythm method!

VICE-POPE: Ah, but only because it doesn't work.

PYTHON: But are you not worried that the population explosion may lead to

THE PYTHON PANEL

greater poverty, disease and eventually war?

VICE-POPE: Well, you must remember, our concern is for the next world. So the quicker we can get people there the better.

FRAMPTON: Your vice-holiness, can you advise me how I should tell Eddie about sex. Whenever I try to bring the subject up casually, he becomes embarrassed.

VICE-POPE: Well, frankly, it's not easy. I mean, take the sex act. Please. *(Laughter)* Well, none of us can work out what God must have been thinking of when He dreamed it up. I mean...you know what people actually do, do you? It's a mind boggler isn't it! Going to the lavatory is bad enough, but...

PYTHON: Vice-Pope, did Christ himself say anything about sex being sinful?

VICE-POPE: Apparently not, no. This was obviously an oversight on his part, which fortunately we have been able to rectify, with the help of the teachings of Paul ...

PYTHON: Oh, the pouf.

FRAMPTON: Does this necessity to sub-edit Christ sometimes worry you?

VICE-POPE: Not really. After all, you can't treat the New Testament as gospel. And one must remember that Christ, though he was a fine young man with some damn good ideas, did go off the rails now and again, rich-man-eye-of-

camel, for example.

KRASZT: But with certain exceptions, you accept his teaching?

VICE-POPE: Oh yes, it's been an invaluable basis for our whole operation really. Of course people accuse us of not practising what we preach, but you must remember that if you're trying to propagate a creed of poverty, gentleness and tolerance, you need a very rich, powerful organisation to do it.

FRAMPTON: I'm afraid I must go now, I have to get Eddie's tea ready.

PYTHON: Well, we've almost finished.

STALIN: But I want to tell you about being Joe Stalin's elder brother. What it felt like to grow up in a family where a tiny child was organising purges all the time! The knock at the nursery door in the middle of the night, the way Joe got rid of Dad and had Auntie Vanya installed as a puppet-father, how he got our smallest sister, Catherina, made eldest brother by giving the dog a vote! How can I tell all that in seven lines?

PYTHON: Six.

STALIN: Well I soon realised the way things were going after all the shooting at Boris's Christening, so I packed my worldly goods and with jaunty step set off for the legendary city of Dundee, in Scotland.

PYTHON: Sorry. That's it.

STALIN: Can't I go on down here?
PYTHON: No. It doesn't look nice.

LARCH
IN COURT

JUDGE: Mr Larch, is there anything you wish to say before I pass sentence?

PRISONER: Well ... I'd just like to say, m'lud, I've got a family ... a wife and six kids ... and I hope very much you don't have to take away my freedom ... because ... well, freedom is a state much prized within the realm of civilised society. It is a bond wherewith the savage man may charm the outward hatchments of his soul, and soothe the troubled breast into a magnitude of quiet. It is most precious as a blessed balm, the saviour of princes, the harbinger of happiness, yea, the very stuff and pith of all we hold most dear. What frees the prisoner in his lonely cell, chained within the bondage of rude walls, far the from the owl of Thebes? What fires and stirs the woodcock in his springe or wakes the drowsy apricot betides? What goddess doth the storm toss'd mariner offer her most tempestuous prayers to? Freedom! Freedom!! Freedom!!!

JUDGE: It's only a bloody parking offence.

COUNSEL: I'm sorry I'm late m'lud, I couldn't find a kosher car park. Please don't bother to recap, I'll pick it up as we go along. Call Mrs Fiona Lewis.

CLERK OF THE COURT: Call Mrs Fiona Lewis!

MRS LEWIS: I swear to tell the truth, the whole truth and nothing but the truth, so *anyway*, I said to her, I said, they can't afford that on what he earns, I mean for a start the feathers get up your nose, I ask you, four and six a pound, and him with a wooden leg, I don't know how she puts up with it after all the trouble she's had with her you-know-what, anyway it was a white wedding much to everyone's surprise, of course they bought everything on the hire purchase, I think they ought to send them back where they came from, I mean you've got to be cruel to be kind so Mrs Harris said, so she said, she said, dead crab she said, she said!

287

Well, her sister's gone to Rhodesia what with her womb and all, and her youngest, her youngest as thin as a filing cabinet, and the goldfish, the goldfish they've got whooping cough they keep spitting water all over their Bratbys, well they do don't they, I mean you *can't* can you, I mean they're not even married or anything, they're not even *divorced*, and he's in the KGB if you ask me, he says that he's a tree surgeon but I don't like the sound of his liver, all that squeaking and banging every night till the small hours, his mother's been much better since she had her head off, yes she has, I said, don't you talk to me about bladders, I said...

MRS LEWIS is carried out of court still talking.

JUDGE: Mr Bartlett, I fail to see the relevance of your last witness.

COUNSEL: My next witness will explain that if m'ludship will allow. Call the late Arthur Aldridge.

JUDGE: The *late* Arthur Aldridge?

JUDGE: Is your witness dead?

COUNSEL: Well ... virtually, m'lud.

JUDGE: He's not completely dead?

COUNSEL: No he's not completely dead m'lud. But he's not at all well.

JUDGE: But if he's not dead, what's he doing in a coffin?

COUNSEL: Oh, it's purely a precaution m'lud – if I may continue? Mr Aldridge, you were a ... you *are* a stockbroker of 10 Savundra Close, Wimbledon.

There is a sound of a knock from the coffin

JUDGE: What was that knock?

COUNSEL: It means 'yes' m'lud. One knock for 'yes', and two knocks for 'no'. Mr Aldridge, would it be fair to say that you are not at all well?

Another knock is heard

In fact Mr Aldridge, not to put too fine a point on it, would you be prepared to say that you are, as it were, what is generally known as, in a manner of speaking, 'dead'? Mr Aldridge I put it to you that you are dead.

COUNSEL: No further questions m'lud.

JUDGE: What do you mean, no further questions? You can't just dump a dead body in my court and say 'no further questions'. I demand an explanation.

COUNSEL: There are no easy answers in this case m'lud.

JUDGE: You haven't the slightest idea what this case is about.

COUNSEL: M'lud, the strange, damnable, almost diabolic threads of this extraordinary tangled web of intrigue will shortly, m'lud, reveal a plot so fiendish, so infernal, so heinous...

JUDGE: Mr Bartlett, your client has already pleaded guilty to the parking offence.

COUNSEL: Parking offence, schmarking offence, m'lud. We must leave no stone unturned. Call Cardinal Richelieu.
JUDGE: Cardinal Richelieu?!?!

CARDINAL: 'Allo everyone, it's wonderful to be 'ere y'know, I just love your country. London is so beautiful at this time of year.
COUNSEL: You are Cardinal Armand du Plessis de Richelieu, First Minister of Louis XIII?
CARDINAL: Oui.
COUNSEL: Cardinal, would it be fair to say that you not only built up the centralized monarchy in France but also perpetuated the religious schism in Europe?
CARDINAL: That's what they say.
COUNSEL: Did you persecute the Huguenots and take even sterner measures against the great Catholic nobles who made common cause with foreign foes in defence of their feudal independence?
CARDINAL: I sure did that thing.
COUNSEL: Speaking as a Cardinal of the Roman Catholic Church, as

First Minister of Louis XIII, and as one of the architects of the modern world already – would you say that Harold Larch was a man of good character?

CARDINAL: Listen! Harry is a very wonderful human being.

Enter INSPECTOR DIM.

DIM: Not so fast!

PRISONER: Why not?

DIM: Well, I'm Dim.

ALL: Dim of the Yard!!

DIM: Yes, and I've a few questions I'd like to ask Cardinal so-called Richelieu.

CARDINAL: Bonjour, Monsieur Dim.

DIM: So-called Cardinal, I put it to you that you died in December 1642.

CARDINAL: That is correct.

DIM: Ah ha! He fell for my little trap.

The court applauds and the CARDINAL *looks dismayed*.

COUNSEL: My life you're clever, Dim. He'd certainly taken me in

DIM: It's all in a day's work.

JUDGE: With a brilliant mind like yours, Dim, you could be something other than a policeman.

DIM: Yes.

JUDGE: What?

DIM *(singing)*: If I were not in the CID

Something else I'd like to be

If I were not in the CID

A window cleaner, me!

JUDGE: Silence! The fine is thirty shillings. Court adjourned.

FEAR NO MAN!

I'll make you a MASTER of LLAP-Goch

...the Secret Welsh ART of SELF DEFENCE that requires NO INTELLIGENCE, STRENGTH or PHYSICAL COURAGE.

The FANTASTIC SECRETS of the SECRET world-famous method of SELF-DEFENCE, kept secret for centuries because of their DEADLY POWER to MAIM, KILL, SMASH, BATTER, FRACTURE, CRUSH, DISMEMBER, CRACK, DISEMBOWEL, CRIPPLE, SNAP are now revealed to YOU in the English Language by a LLAP-GOCH master AT HIS OWN RISK, PROVIDED you promise to MAIM, CRUSH, DISEMBOWEL and so on ONLY in SELF DEFENCE.* *This is just to cover ourselves, as you will understand.

WHO IS THIS MAN ? This is the LLAP-GOCH MASTER who will reveal to YOU the SECRETS of LAPP. GOCH HE IS A FULLY QUALIFIED leek-coloured BELT FIRST DAI MASTER and cares nothing for the penal reform.

WHY "At his own risk"?

BECAUSE if his fellow masters of LLAP-GOCH DISCOVER his IDENTITY, they will PUNISH HIM SEVERELY for revealing the DEADLY secrets he had promised to keep SECRET, without giving them a piece of the ACTION, and also BECAUSE of the TERRIBLE risk of PUNISHMENT he runs under the Trades Description Act.

WHAT is LLAP-GOCH?

IT is THE most DEADLY form of SECRET self-DEFENCE that HAS ever been widely advertised and available to EVERYONE.

WHY ALL the CAPITALS?

Because THE most likely kind of person TO answer THIS kind of advertisement HAS less trouble under-STANDING words if they ARE written in BIG letters.

WHAT is LLAP-GOCH again?

It is an ANCIENT Welsh ART based on a BRILLIANTLY simple I-D-E-A, that the most VITAL element of ATTACK is SURPRISE Therefore ... the BEST way to protect yourself AGAINST any ASSAILANT is to ATTACK him before he attacks YOU... Or BETTER ... BEFORE the THOUGHT of doing so has EVEN OCCURRED TO HIM!!!

SO YOU MAY BE ABLE TO RENDER YOUR ASSAILENT *UNCONSCIOUS* BEFORE He is even aware of your very existance!

BANISH INADEQUACY

No longer need you feel WEAK, helpless, INDECISIVE, NOT fascinating and ASHAMED of your genital dimentions. No more need you be out-manoeuvred in political debate!! GOOD BYE HUMILIATION, Wisecracking bullies, Karate experts, boxing champions, sarcastic vicars, traffic wardens, entire panzer divisions will melt to pulp as you master every situation without INADEQUACY. PROTECT YOUR LOVED ONES. You will no longer look pitiful and spotty to your GIRL FRIENDS when you leave some unsuspecting passer-by 'looking like four tins of cat food'. They will admire you for your MASTERY and DECISIVENESS and LACK OF you for your MASTERY and DECISIVENESS and LACK OF INADEQUACY and will almost certainly let you put your HAND inside their BLOUSE out of sheer ADMIRATION and after seeing more of your expert disabling they'll almost definitely go to bed with you .

Why WELSH Art?

Llap-Goch was developed in Wales because for the average Welshman, the best prospects of achieving a reasonable standard of living lie with the aquisition of the most efficient techniques of armed robbery.

How do I learn?

No, you mean 'How do *you* learn'. I know already

How do you learn?

You receive ABSOLUTELY FREE your own special personal LLAP-GOCH Picture Book with hundreds of PHOTOGRAPHS and just very few plain, clear and simple, easy to understand words.

Only a FOUR-SECOND WORK OUT Each Day!

and you will be ready to HARM people, DEVELOP UP TO 38" BICEPS, GROW UP TO 12" TALLER, LOSE UP TO 40" OF FAT IN YOUR FIRST WORK-OUT! PROLONG YOUR LIFE BY *UP TO* 1,000 YEARS. GO TO BED WITH UP TO ANY LUDICROUS NUMBER OF GIRLS YOU CARE TO THINK OF PROVIDING YOU REALISE THIS STATEMENT IS QUITE MEANINGLESS AS THE PHRASE UP TO' CLEARLY INCLUDES THE NUMBER 'NOUGHT'.

What Does it Cost?

This, like LLAP-GOCH, is a SECRET but you will find out sooner or later, don't worry.

THE
MERCHANT BANKER

COLLECTOR: Thank you for seeing me. My name is Phillips.

BANKER: How do you do. I'm a merchant banker.

COLLECTOR: How do you do Mr...

BANKER: Er ... I forget my name for the moment, but I am a merchant banker.

COLLECTOR: I wondered whether you'd like to contribute to the orphans' home.

BANKER: Well actually here at Slater Nazi we are quite keen to get into orphans, you know, developing market and all that ... what sort of sum did you have in mind?

COLLECTOR: Well ... er ... you're a rich man.

BANKER: Yes, I am. Yes. Yes, very very rich. Quite phenomenally wealthy. I do own the most startling quantities of cash. Yes, quite right ... you're a smart young lad aren't you?

COLLECTOR: Thank you, sir.

BANKER: Now, as you were saying, I'm very, very, very, very, very, very, very, very, very, very rich.

COLLECTOR: So er, how about a pound?

BANKER: A pound. Yes, I see. Now this loan would be secured by the ...

COLLECTOR: It's not a loan, sir.

BANKER : What?

COLLECTOR: It's not a loan.

BANKER: Ah.

COLLECTOR: You get one of these little flags, sir.

BANKER: It's a bit small for a share certificate isn't it? Look, I think I'd better run this over to our legal department. If you could possibly pop back on Friday.

COLLECTOR: Well do you have to do that, couldn't you just give me the pound?

BANKER: Yes, but you see I don't know what it's *for*.

COLLECTOR: It's for the orphans.

BANKER: ...Yes.

COLLECTOR: It's a gift.

BANKER: A what?

COLLECTOR: A gift.

BANKER: Oh a *gift!* A tax dodge.

COLLECTOR: No, no, no, no.

BANKER: No? Well, I'm awfully sorry I don't understand. Can you just explain exactly what you want?

COLLECTOR: Well, I want you to give me a pound, and then I go away and give it to the orphans.

BANKER: Go on.

COLLECTOR: Well, that's it.

BANKER: ...No, no, no, I don't follow this at all, I mean, I don't want to seem stupid but it looks to me as though I'm a pound down on the whole deal.

COLLECTOR: Well, yes you are.

BANKER: I *am!* Well, what is my incentive to give you the pound?

COLLECTOR: Well the incentive is – to make the orphans happy.

BANKER: Are you quite sure you've got this right?

COLLECTOR: Yes, *lots* of people give me money.

BANKER: What, just like that?

COLLECTOR: Yes.

BANKER: Must be sick. I don't suppose you could give me a list of their names and addresses could you?

COLLECTOR: No, I just go up to them in the street and ask.

BANKER: Good lord! That's the most exciting new idea I've heard in years! It's so simple it's brilliant! Well, if that idea of yours isn't worth a pound I'd like to know what is.

COLLECTOR: Oh, thank you sir.

BANKER: The only trouble is, you gave me the idea before I'd given you the pound. And that's not good business.

COLLECTOR: Isn't it?

BANKER: No I'm afraid it isn't. So, off you go!

He presses a button

BANKER: Nice to do business with you.

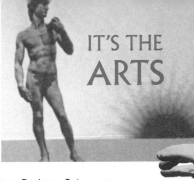

Johann
What's-His-Name

PRESENTER: Beethoven, Mozart, Chopin, Liszt, Brahms, Schumann, Schubert, Mendelssohn and Bach. Names that will live forever. But there is one composer whose name is never included with the greats. Why is it that the world has never remembered the name of Johann Gambolputty de von Ausfernschpledenschlittcrasscrenbonfriedig-gordingledangledongleburgsteinvonknackerthrasherapplebanger-horowitzticolensicgranderknottyspelltinklegrandlichgrumblemeyer-spelterwasserkurstlichhimbleeisenbahnwagengutenabendbitteein-nürnburgerbratwurstlegerspurtemitzweimacheluberhundsfütgumber-aberschönendankerkalbsfleischmittleraucher Von Hautkopft of Ulm?

To do justice to this man, thought by many to be the greatest name in German Baroque music, we present tonight a profile of Jo-hann Gambolputty de von Ausfernschpledenschlittcrasscrenbon-friediggerdingledangledongleburgsteinvonknackerthrasherapple-bangerhorowitzticolensicgranderknottyspelltinklegrandlichgrumble-meyerspelterwasserkurstlichhimbleeisenbahnwagengutenabendbit-teeinürnburgerbratwurstlegerspurtenmitzweimacheluberhundsfüt-gumberaberschönendankerkalbsfleischmittleraucher von Hautkopft of Ulm. We start with an interview with his only surviving relative, his greatnephew, Karl, who is talking to Al Fry.

KARL: Oh ja. When I first met Johann Gambolputty de von Ausfernsch-pledenschlittcrasscrenbonfriediggerdingledangledongleburgstein-vonknackerthrasherapplebangerhorowitzticolensicgranderknot-

tyspelltinklegrandlichgrumblemeyerspelterwasserkurstlichhimbleeisenbahnwagengutenabendbitteeinürnburgerbratwurstlegerspurtenmitzweimacheluberhundsütgumberaberschönendankerkalbsfleischmittleraucher von Hautkopft of Ulm, he was with his wife, Sarah Gambolputty de von Ausfernschpledenschlittcrass...

INTERVIEWER: Yes, if I may just cut in on you there, Herr Gambolputty de von Ausfernschpledenschlittcrasscrenbonfriediggerdingledangledonglebursteinvonknackerthrasherapplebangerhorowitzticolensicgranderknottyspelltinklegrandlichgrumblemeyerspelterwasserkurstlichhimbleeisenbahnwagengutenabendbitteeinürnburgerbratwurstlegerspurtenmitzweimacheluberhundsfütgumberaberschönendankerkalbsfleischmittleraucher von Hautkopft of Ulm, and ask you – just quickly – if there's any particular thing that you remember about Johann Gambolputty de von Ausfernschpledenschlittcrasscrenbonfriediggerdingledangledonglebursteinvonknackerthrasherapplebangerhorowitzticolensicgranderknottyspelltinklegrandlichgrumblemeyerspelterwasserkurstlichhimbleeisenbahnwagengutenabendbitteeinürnburgerbratwurstlegerspurtenmitzweimacheluberhundsfütgumberaberschönendankerkalbsfleischmittleraucher von Hautkopft of Ulm?

Hallo?

The Last Supper

POPE: Good evening, Michelangelo.

MICHELANGELO: Evening, your holiness.

POPE: I want to have a word with you about this 'Last Supper' of yours.

MICHELANGELO: Yes?

POPE: I'm not happy with it.

MICHELANGELO: Oh, dear. It took hours.

POPE: Not happy at all…

MICHELANGELO: Do the jellies worry you? They add a bit of colour, don't they? Oh, I know – you don't like the kangaroo.

POPE: … What kangaroo?

MICHELANGELO: I'll alter it, no sweat.

POPE: I never saw a kangaroo!

MICHELANGELO: It's right at the back, I'll paint it out, no problem. I'll make it into a disciple.

POPE: Ah!

MICHELANGELO: All right now?

POPE: That's the problem.

MICHELANGELO: … What is?

POPE: The disciples.

MICHELANGELO: Are they too Jewish? I made Judas the most Jewish.

POPE: No, no, it's just that there are twenty-eight of them.

MICHELANGELO: Well, another one would hardly notice, then.

POPE: No!!

MICHELANGELO: All right, all right, we'll lose the kangaroo altogether – I don't mind, I was never completely happy with it …

POPE: That's not the point. There are twenty-eight disciples.

MICHELANGELO: ...Too many?

POPE: Of course it's too many!

MICHELANGELO: Well, in a way, but I wanted to give the impression of a huge get-together ... you know, a real Last Supper – not any old supper, but a proper final treat...

POPE: There were only twelve disciples at the Last Supper.

MICHELANGELO: ... Supposing some of the others happened to drop by?

POPE: There were only twelve altogether.

MICHELANGELO: Well, maybe they'd invited some friends?

POPE: There were only twelve disciples and Our Lord at the Last Supper. The Bible clearly says so.

MICHELANGELO: ... No friends?

POPE: No friends.

MICHELANGELO: ... Waiters?

POPE: No!

MICHELANGELO: ... Cabaret?

POPE: No!!

MICHELANGELO: ... You see, I like them. They fill out the canvas. I mean, I suppose we could lose three or four of them, you know, make them...

POPE: There were only twelve disciples and our Lord at the Last ...

MICHELANGELO: I've got it, I've got it!!! We'll call it ... 'The Penultimate Supper'. The Bible doesn't say how many people there were at that, does it?

POPE: Er, no, but ...

MICHELANGELO: Well, there you are, then!

POPE: Look!! The Last Supper is a significant event in the life of

Our Lord. The Penultimate Supper was not, even if they had a conjurer and a steel band. Now I commissioned a Last Supper from you, and a Last Supper I want …

MICHELANGELO: Yes, but look …

POPE: … With twelve disciples and one Christ!

MICHELANGELO: … One?!

POPE: Yes, one. Now will you please tell me what in God's name possessed you to paint this with *three* Christs in it?

MICHELANGELO: It works, mate!!

POPE: It does not work!

MICHELANGELO: It does, it looks great! The fat one balances the two skinny ones!

POPE: There was only one Saviour …

MICHELANGELO: I know that, but what about a bit of artistic licence?

POPE: One Redeemer …

MICHELANGELO: I'll tell you what you want, mate, you want a bloody photographer, not a creative artist with some imagination!!

POPE: I'll tell you what I want – I want a Last Supper, with one Christ, twelve disciples, no kangaroos, by Thursday lunch, or you don't get paid!!

MICHELANGELO: You fascist!!

POPE: Look, I'm the bloody Pope I am! I may not know much about art, but I know what I like …

TOASTMASTER: Gentlemen, pray silence for the President of the Royal Society for Putting Things on Top of Other Things.

SIR WILLIAM: I thank you, gentlemen. The year has been a good one for the Society

(Cries of 'hear hear')

This year our members have put more things on top of other things than ever before. But, I should warn you, this is no time for complacency. No, there are still many things, and I cannot emphasize this too strongly, not on top of other things. I myself, on my way here this evening, saw a thing that was not on top of another thing in any way.

(Cries of 'shame')

Shame indeed, but we must not allow ourselves to become despondent. For we must never forget that if there was not one thing that was not on top of another thing, our society would be nothing more than a meaningless body of men that had gathered together for no good purpose. But we flourish. This year our Australasian members and the various organizations affiliated to our Australasian branches put no fewer than twenty-two things on top of other things.

(Applause)

Well done all of you. But there is one cloud on the horizon. In this last year our Staffordshire branch has not succeeded in putting one thing on top ...

(and so on, and so on, and so on, and so on, and so on, and so on, and so on, an

304

ARTHUR
'TWO SHEDS' JACKSON

INTERVIEWER: Last week the Royal Festival Hall saw the first performance of a new symphony by one of the world's leading modern composers, Arthur 'Two Sheds' Jackson. Mr Jackson, welcome.

JACKSON: Good evening.

INTERVIEWER: May I sidetrack you for one moment Mr Jackson, and ask about this nickname of yours.

JACKSON: Oh yes.

INTERVIEWER: 'Two Sheds'. How did you come by it?

JACKSON: Well I don't use it myself, it's just a few of my friends call me 'Two Sheds'.

INTERVIEWER: I see, and do you in fact have two sheds?

JACKSON: No. No, I've only one shed I've had one for some time, but a few years ago I said I was thinking of getting another one and since then some people have called me 'Two Sheds'.

INTERVIEWER: In spite of the fact that you have only one.

JACKSON: Exactly.

INTERVIEWER: I see. And are you still thinking of purchasing a second shed?

JACKSON: No.

INTERVIEWER: I see, I see. Well let's return to your symphony. Now did you write this symphony ... *in* your shed?

JACKSON: ...No!

INTERVIEWER: Have you written any of your recent works in this shed of yours?

JACKSON: No. It's an ordinary garden shed.

INTERVIEWER: So were you thinking of buying this second shed to write in?

JACKSON: No, look, this shed business, it doesn't really matter at all, the sheds aren't important. It's just a few friends call me 'Two Sheds', and that's all there is to it. I wish you'd ask me about my music. People always ask me about the sheds, they've got it out of proportion, I'm fed up with the shed, I wish I'd never got it in the first place.

INTERVIEWER: Are you thinking of selling it?

JACKSON: Yes.

INTERVIEWER: Then you'd be Arthur 'No Sheds' Jackson!

JACKSON: Look, forget about the sheds! They don't matter!!!

Enter SECOND INTERVIEWER

SECOND INTERVIEWER: Are you having any trouble from him?

INTERVIEWER: A little.

SECOND INTERVIEWER: Well, we interviewers are more than a match for the likes of you, 'Two Sheds'.

INTERVIEWER: Yes make yourself scarce, 'Two Sheds'! This studio isn't big enough for the three of us.

SECOND INTERVIEWER: Get your own arts programme, you fairy!

WORD ASSOCIATION FOOTBALL

GOOD EVENING. TONIGHT'S THE NIGHT I SHALL BE TALKING ABOUT OF 'FLU
THE SUBJECT OF WORD ASSOCIATION FOOTBALL. THIS IS A TECHNIQUE
OUT A LIVING MUCH USED IN THE PRACTICE MAKES PERFECT OF
PSYCHOANALYSISTER AND BROTHER AND ONE THAT HAS OCCUPIED PIPER
THE MAJORITY RULE OF MY ATTENTION SQUAD BY THE RIGHT NUMBER ONE
TWO THREE FOUR THE LAST FIVE YEARS TO THE MEMORY. IT IS QUITE
REMARKABLEBAKERCHARLIE HOW MUCH THE MILLER'S SON THIS SO
CALLED WHILE YOU WERE OUT WORD ASSOCIATION IMMIGRANTS' PROBLEMS
INFLUENCES THE MANNER FROM HEAVEN IN WHICH WE SLEEKIT COWERIN
TIMROUS BEASTIES ALL-AMERICAN SPEKE THE FAMOUS EXPLORER. AND THI
REALLY WELL THAT IS SURPRISING PARTNER IN CRIME IS THAT A LOT AND HIS
WIFE OF THE LIONS' FEEDINGTIME WE MAY BE C D E EFFECTIVELY QUITE
UNAWARE OF THE FACT OR FICTION SECTION OF THE WATFORD PUBLIC
LIBRARY THAT WE ARE EVEN DOING IT IS A FAR, FAR BETTER THING THAT I DO
NOW THEN, NOW THEN, WHAT'S GOING ONWARD CHRISTIAN BARNARD THE
FAMOUS HEARTY PART OF THE LETTUCE NOW PRAISE FAMOUS MENTA
HOMES FOR LOONIES. LIKE ME. SO MY CONTENTION CAUSING ALL THE
HEADACHES, IS THAT UNLESS WE TAKE INTO ACCOUNT OF MONTE-CRISTO IN
OUR THINKING GEORGE V THIS PHENOMENON THE OTHER HAND WE SHALL
NOT BE ABLE SATISFACT OR FICTIONSECTION OF THE WATFORD PUBLIC
LIBRARYAGAINILY TO UNDERSTAND TO ATTENTION WHEN I'M TALKING TO YOU
AND STOP LAUGHING, ABOUT HUMAN NATURE, MAN'S PSYCHOLOGICA
MAKE-UP SOME STORY THE WIFE'LL BELIEVE AND HENCE THE VERY MEANING
OF LIFE ITSELFISH BASTARD I'LL KICK HIM IN THE BALL'S POND ROAD

NORMAN HENDERSON'S DIARY

Edited by Eric Henderson

Norman Henderson began keeping a diary on March 21st 1956. He continued to write that diary every day without fail until the day he died. As he himself puts it in that first entry: 'I have decided to keep ... a personal record ... of my most intimate thoughts'. He undertook this mammoth task, as I remember he undertook most things in his life, simply and uncomplainingly. He lived in a time when much was happening at home and abroad, and his diary is interesting historically for the way in which it reflects one man's reaction to his times, *at the time*. In a diary there is no benefit from hindsight – this is its strength as much as its weakness and here everything is reflected in the way it seemed then, without the perspective of distance.

Eric Henderson, Leicester, 1971

HISTORICAL NOTE

1956 was indeed a 'year of change', the title Norman Henderson adopted at the beginning of his diary for that year. Perhaps the high water mark of old-style Conservative government, under Sir Anthony Eden, England was shortly to plunge into the new world of Macmillan in the wake of the mammoth upheavals of the world around. On the home front it was the year of Princess Margaret's Caribbean Tour and the State Visit of King Haakon of Norway. Monsieur P. Wertheimer's Lavandin won the Derby, England won the Ashes with fine victories at Headingly and Trent Bridge, and Cambridge won the Boat Race for the 56th time.

1956 A YEAR OF CHANGE

Wednesday March 21st

I have been reading a lot of Harold Nicholson recently and have decided to keep a diary. It will be a personal record of my daily actions and my most intimate thoughts. Since I know most of the leading figures of the day, my experience of them too, may be of interest when my grandchildren come to read this account of an ordinary man in mid-twentieth century England.

Breakfasted with Peter [Thorneycroft], Selwyn [Lloyd] and Nathaniel [Jackley] whom I had specially invited to meet the others. They were alarmed at first by his sudden movements but thought his Suez invasion plan a good one if only the French and Israelis would agree.

Later visited Harrods. Went to Food Hall and bought up every single prawn they had! My, how they scurried about when I demanded to see the stock rooms in case they had missed one! Then crammed them all in a taxi and told cabbie to deliver to J. B. Priestley. I know he likes them. Bumped into Queen Juliana in the Electrical Department, buying bulbs. She in top form and ate one! Then I chased her down escalator pretending we were loonies. What a good sport she is!

Lunch with Hailsham and – [Civil Servant]. Asked – why he didn't have a name. He said it was hereditary; also very useful for tax purposes. After lunch were joined by Marquis of Salisbury so went to St James's Park in our badger outfits and hid behind bushes jumping out at civil servants. What a stuffy lot they are! One had a heart attack and a policeman was called; so we had to bribe him.

Went to first night of Three Sisters at Haymarket with Daphne and the Astors. Sat behind Lord Brabazon and next to Duchess of Argyll. Rather slow third act so we [N.H. *and* D.H. - Ed.] went up on stage and ran about a bit, causing quite a stir. We stopped when Tchebutykin's big soliloquy came, though, and sat down by him so as not to spoil people's enjoyment. What a sad speech it is! When it was over, though, we were up again, pushing the characters over till they had to bring the curtain down.

Went on to first night party afterwards. People seemed a little cool and the German ambassador scowled at us. Fucking Kraut. Who won the war? Felt rather depressed so stuffed pâté up my nose which cheered me up a lot. Then Queen Soraya arrived and I sneezed at worst possible moment. Then threw up over Duke of Norfolk. What a day! Went home and early bed but heard on news that Italy had annexed Yugoslavia. Later transpired it was a joke. Poor old BBC! Nothing they do is right.

Thursday March 22nd

Woke up late and read our reviews. Rather mixed.

At breakfast I had an innermost thought. How would horses run if they only had two legs, one at each end? A sort of rumba I suppose. Depressed me all morning.

Lunched with Duncan [Sandys], Heathcoat [Amory] and Reggie [Maudling] at Beefsteak. Duncan says Tony Chatsworth [Minister of Defence] is finished and must go [T.C. had at this point been dead for over four months - Ed.] Reggie agreed but said we must wait till after bye-elections [Nov 14th].

3 o'clock. Cabinet meeting. P.M. not looking at all well. Pale and drawn and wearing cork hat. Also cries a lot. Asked me what I thought about cheese. What could I say? I replied that it was reliable enough stuff but that he should not count on it in an emergency. He seemed satisfied by this but Barbara [Windsor] thought it v. funny. She is a nice enough lady but must be a risk at the Board of Trade. Eventually meeting finished. Sad to see PM

in this state. Just yodels to himself and makes faces in mirror. Also incontinent. And yet he is the best man we have! I was also surprised to find how easy it had been to get into a cabinet meeting. A lot of foreigners there too.

Met Harold [Macmillan] and Lady Violet [Bonham-Carter] at Moo-Cow in Greek Street. Harold said crisis was on us but felt it best to keep it from nation in case they got annoyed. Baited waitress.

Tea at the Mcnuhins. A lot of fighting as usual. Took taxi home in nude but was involved in an accident with a lorry in Oxford Street. Was quite badly hurt and had to travel in ambulance to hospital. Died before we got there, though.

Friday March 23rd

Nothing much. Funeral arranged for tomorrow. Rather depressed.

Saturday March 24th

Service at St Thomas, Belgravia.
Then on to cemetery.
Buried about 11.15 a.m.

KING ARTHUR AND HIS KNIGHTS ARE OVERJOYED TO REACH THE CASTLE.

The Sacred Castle

SUDDENLY A VOICE COMES FROM THE BATTLEMENTS...

FROG: Hello smelly English kerniggets ... and Monsieur Arthur King, who has the brain of a duck, y'know. We French persons outwit you a second time, perfidious English mousedropping hoarders, begorrah!

ARTHUR: How dare you profane this place with your presence! I command you, in the name of the Knights of Camelot, open the door to the Sacred Castle to which God himself has guided us!

FROG: How you English say, I one more time, mac, unclog my nose towards you, sons of a window-dresser! So you think you could out-clever us French fellows with your silly knees-bent creeping about advancing behaviour. I wave my private parts at your aunties, you brightly-coloured, cranberry-smelling, electric donkey-bottom biters.

ARTHUR: In the name of our Lord, we demand entrance to the Sacred Castle.

FROG: No chance, English bed-wetting types. We burst our pimples at you, and call your door-opening request a silly thing. You tiny-brained wipers of other people's bottoms.

Much French laughter.

ARTHUR: If you do not open these doors, we will take the castle by force ...

A bucket of what can only be described as human waste hits ARTHUR, ARTHUR leads the knights away. French jeering follows them.

FROG: Yes, depart a lot at this time, and cut the approaching any more or we fire arrows into the tops of your heads and make castanets of your testicles already. Your mother was a hamster and your father smelt of elderberries.

ARTHUR (*to KNIGHTS*): Just ignore him.

A small hail of chickens, watercress, badgers and mattresses lands on them.

FROG: And now remain gone, illegitimate-faced bugger-folk! And if you think you got a nasty taunting this time, you ain't heard nothing yet, dappy kerniggets and A.King Esquire.

SPOT THE SPECIES

A. RED-RUFFED LEMUR
B. MOUSE LEMUR
C. WHITE-FRONTED LEMUR
D. RING-TAILED LEMUR
E. COQUEREL'S SIFAKA
F. HURLEY'S LEMUR
G. GENTLE LEMUR
H. DWARF LEMUR
I. MONGOOSE LEMUR

DOCUMENTARY

MRS JALIN: There's a man at the door.

MR JALIN: What's he want?

MRS JALIN: He says do we want a documentary on molluscs.

MR JALIN: What's he mean, molluscs?

MRS JALIN: MOLLUSCS!! GASTROPODS! LAMELLIBRANCHS! CEPHALOPODS!

MR JALIN: Oh, molluscs. What's he charge then?

MRS JALIN: It's free.

MR JALIN: Ooh! Where does he want us to sit?

ZORBA: Good morning. Tonight molluscs. The mollusc is a soft-bodied, unsegmented invertebrate animal usually protected by a large shell. One of the most numerous groups of invertebrates, it is exceeded in number of species only by the arthropods viz, this lobster.

MRS JALIN: Not very interesting is it?

ZORBA: What?

MRS JALIN: I was talking to my husband.

ZORBA: Oh. Anyway, the typical mollusc, viz, this snail, consists of a prominent muscular portion, the head-foot, a visceral mass and a shell which is secreted by the free edge of the mantle.

MRS JALIN: Dreadful isn't it?

ZORBA: ... What?

MRS JALIN: I was talking to him.

ZORBA: Oh. Well anyway ... in some molluscs, however, viz, this slug, the shell is absent or rudimentary ...

MR JALIN: Switch him off.

MRS JALIN *gets up and looks for the switch.*

ZORBA: Whereas in others, viz, cephalopods, the head-foot is greatly modified and forms tentacles, viz, the squid. What are you doing?

MRS JALIN: Switching you off.

ZORBA: Why, don't you like it?

MRS JALIN: Oh it's dreadful.

MR JALIN: Embarrassing.

ZORBA: ...Is it?

MR JALIN: I don't know how they've got the nerve to put it on.

MRS JALIN: It's so boring.

ZORBA: Well, it's not much of a subject is it? Be fair.

MRS JALIN: What do you think, George?

MR JALIN: Give him another twenty seconds.

ZORBA: Anyway the majority of the molluscs are included in three large groups , the gastropods, the lamellibranchs and the cephalopods.

MRS JALIN: We *know* that.

MR JALIN: Switch him off!

ZORBA: However, what is more interesting, is the mollusc's sex life.

MRS JALIN : ... Oh!

ZORBA: Yes, the mollusc is a randy little fellow whose primitive brain scarcely strays from the subject of you-know-what.

MRS JALIN : Disgusting!

ZORBA : The randiest of the gastro-pods is the limpet. This hot-blooded little beast with its tent-like shell is always on the job. Its extra-marital activities are something startling. Frankly I don't know how the female limpet finds the time to adhere to the rock-face. How am I doing?

319

MRS JALIN: It's disgusting.

MR JALIN: But more interesting.

MRS JALIN: Oh yes. Tch, tch, tch, tch, tch, tch.

ZORBA: Another loose-living gastropod is the periwinkle. This shameless little libertine with its characteristic ventral locomotion is not the marrying kind. 'Anywhere, anytime' is its motto. Up with the shell and they're at it.

MRS JALIN: How about the lamellibranchs?

ZORBA: I'm coming to them. Take the scallop This tatty, scrofulous old rapist, is second in depravity only to the common clam. This latter is a right whore, a harlot, a trollop, a cynical bed-hopping firm-breasted Rabelaisian bit of sea food that makes Fanny Hill look like a dead pope. And finally among the bivalves, that most depraved of the whole sub-species – the whelk. The whelk is nothing but a homosexual of the worst kind. This gay boy of the gastropods, this queer crustacean, this mincing mollusc, this screaming, prancing, limp-wristed queen of the deep makes me sick.

MRS JALIN: Have you got one?

ZORBA: Here!

MRS JALIN: Let's kill it.

ZORBA throws it on the floor and Mr and Mrs Jalin stamp on it.

MR JALIN: That'll teach it. Well thank you for a very interesting programme.

ZORBA: Oh, not at all. Thank you.

MRS JALIN: Yes, that was very nice.

ZORBA: Thank you.

MR JALIN: Thank *you*.

Chapel

HEADMASTER: And spotteth twice they the camels before the third hour. And so the Midianites went forth to Ram Gilead in Kadesh Bilgemath by Shor Ethra Regalion, to the house of Gash-Bil-Bethuel-Bazda, he who brought the butter dish to Balshazar and the tent peg to the house of Rashomon, and there slew they the goats, yea, and placed they the bits in little pots.
Here endeth the lesson.

CHAPLAIN: Let us praise God. Oh Lord ...
CONGREGATION: Oh Lord ...
CHAPLAIN: Oooh, you are so big ...
CONGREGATION: Oooh, you are so big ...
CHAPLAIN: So absolutely *huge*.
CONGREGATION: So absolutely *huge*.
CHAPLAIN: Gosh, we're all really impressed down here I can tell you.
CONGREGATION: Hear hear!
CHAPLAIN: Forgive us, oh Lord, for this our dreadful toadying.
CONGREGATION: And barefaced flattery.
CHAPLAIN: But you are so strong and, well, just so *super*.
CONGREGATION: Fan-*tastic*!
HEADMASTER: Amen. Now two boys have been found rubbing linseed oil into the school cormorant. Now some of you may feel that the cormorant does not play an important part in the life of the school but I would remind you that it was presented to us by the Corporation of the town of Sudbury to commemorate Empire Day, when we try to

remember the names of all those from the Sudbury area who so gallantly gave their lives to keep China British. So from now on the cormorant is strictly out of bounds. And Jenkins, apparently your mother died this morning.

Oh Lord, please don't burn us,
Don't grill or toast your flock.
Don't put us on the barbecue,
Or simmer us in stock.
Don't braise or bake or boil us,
Or stir-fry us in a wok ...

Oh please don't lightly poach us,
Or baste us with hot fat.
Don't fricassée or roast us,
Or boil us in a vat.
And please don't stick thy servants Lord,
In a Rotissomat ...

INDEX